Fisheries bioeconomics

Theory, modelling and management

by
J. C. Seijo
Departamento de Recursos del Mar
CINVESTAV-IPN Unidad Mérida
Mérida, Yucatán, México,
and Centro Marista de Estudios Superiores
Mérida, Yucatán, México

D. Defeo
Departamento de Recursos del Mar
CINVESTAV-IPN Unidad Merida
Mérida, Yucatán, México,
and Instituto Nacional de Pesca
Montevideo, Uruguay

S. Salas
Departamento de Recursos Del Mar
CINVESTAV-IPN Unidad Mérida
Mérida, Yucatán, México

2001

Reprint by arrangement with the Food and Agriculture Organization of the United Nations

by

DAYA PUBLISHING HOUSE
Delhi–110035

FAO FISHERIES TECHNICAL PAPER

368

Food and Agriculture Organization of the United Nations

FIAT PANIS

Rome, 1998

visit us at : www:dayabooks.com

"This book was originally published by the Food and Agriculture Organization of the United Nations (FAO) as Fisheries Bioeconomics—Theory, Modelling and Management, FAO Fisheries Technical Paper 368.

"The designations employed and the presentation of material in this publication do not imply the expression of any opinion, whatsoever on the part of the Food and Agriculture Organization of the United Nations concerning the legal status of any country, territory, city or area or of its authorities, or concerning the delimitation of its frontiers or boundaries.'

'The designations 'developed' and 'developing' economies are intended for statistical convenience and do not necessarily express a judgement about the stage reached by a particular country, territory or area in the development process.'

First Indian Edition 2001
ISBN 81-7035-250-9

Rs. 450

Published by : Daya Publishing House
1123/74, Deva Ram Park,
Tri Nagar Delhi-110035
Phone : 7103999
Fax : (011) 7198902
e-mail : dayabooks@vsnl.com.

Printed at : Chawla Offset Printers
Delhi-110052

Preparation of this Document

The evaluation and mathematical representation of dynamic trends in populations of fishery resources was originally considered solely in terms of the interaction between the intensity of fishing and the biological constraints that determine the productivity of marine ecosystems. While detailed study of fish population dynamics and fish stock assessment is still valid, the subject of fish population dynamics is progressively being treated in combination with those economic forces driving the dynamics of a fishery, such as rent, human employment and food production. This combined activity is referred to as 'Bioeconomics' and FAO has already issued a number of publications of more specialized software in this area, but has not so far produced a text containing theory and examples of application. The present text fills this void, and focuses particularly on problems faced by developing countries in this field.

Acknowledgements

We wish to express our gratitude to the working group of Fisheries Bioeconomics at CINVESTAV, especially to Miguel Cabrera, Anita de Alava and José Luis Cabrera for their help in the edition of the manuscript. We acknowledge Rögnvaldur Hannesson for his detailed revision of the manuscript and John Caddy for his useful comments and editorial review. Eduardo Pérez helped us in the elaboration of the subject index. Enzo Acuña, Jorge González, Minerva Arce and Eduardo Balart provided valuable comments that improved the text. Héctor Mares elaborated the cover of this book. We wish to express our deepest gratitude for those students who attended the posgraduate course of *Fisheries Bioeconomics* at CINVESTAV-Unidad Mérida (México) and in several Institutions of Latin America, during the last ten years.

Juan Carlos Seijo wish to express his gratitude to Ceci, Juan Carlos Jr. and Adrianita for being a permanent source of motivation and love. Omar Defeo dedicates this book to Anita, Diego, his parents and brothers. Silvia Salas dedicates it to her daughter Nayelli and her parents.

Distribution:

All FAO Members and Associate Members
FAO Fisheries Department
FAO Fishery Officers in FAO Regional Offices
Non-governmental Institutions

Seijo, J.C.; Defeo, O.; Salas, S.
Fisheries bioeconomics. Theory, modelling and management.
***FAO Fisheries Technical Paper.* No. 368. Rome, FAO. 1998. 108p.**

ABSTRACT

This book is presented in seven Chapters. Chapter 1 describes the basic assumptions underlying the optimal allocation of natural resources and the inherent characteristics of fisheries that determine, under unrestricted access, the failure to allocate resources, economic inefficiency and overfishing. To mitigate these undesired effects, the bioeconomic literature invokes the allocation of property rights, which in turn must be implemented within a management context. Thus, in this Chapter we suggest some guidelines to conduct management plans. Static and dynamic bioeconomic models are presented in Chapter 2 as a theoretical framework for the design of intelligent management schemes aiming at sustainable use of fish stocks. Classic models are shown, such as the Gordon-Schaefer based on the logistic. We also develop new bioeconomic approaches, such as a distributed-delay model to add realism to Smith's fleet dynamics approach. Chapter 2 also includes an introductory version of a bioeconomic yield-mortality model, and dynamic age-structured models. A comparison of the dynamic and static trajectories is stressed. The price of time and its implications for optimal resource allocation over time is also discussed. For the sake of adding realism to the above models, the systems approach is used in Chapter 3 to model different technological and ecological complexities that occur in marine fisheries. Ecological interdependencies (competition, predation), as well as technological interdependencies resulting from fleets with different fishing power and/or gear types, operating on components of a stock, or on different target species of a "mixed stock", are specified and modelled. In Chapter 4 we provide practical guidelines for the application of the systems science approach as a systematic and robust methodology for modelling fisheries. We present theory and examples on how to model the short and long run dynamics of the stock and the fishery, including the application of distributed delay models to represent from hatching/spawning processes to intra and interannual dynamics of fishing fleets. Chapter 5 gives an overview of a number of alternative methods for managing fisheries, and develop a bioeconomic approach to fisheries management with multiple criteria, introducing a nonlinear optimization algorithm. In Chapter 6 we relax the dynamic pool assumption of models developed in Chapters 2, 3 and 4 and introduce spatial bioeconomic considerations in modelling fisheries, notably the distance from ports to fishing grounds in order to further understand short-run decision-making of fishers in their allocation of fishing intensity. Stochastic models are detailed, also adding a degree of complexity to the interdependencies discussed in Chapter 3. The incorporation of risk and uncertainty in bioeconomic modelling and a formal decision analysis has been scarcely documented in the fisheries literature. In Chapter 7 we present some alternative ways of contending with risk and uncertainty in a precautionary fishery management context. Some aspects of decision analysis are detailed. Mathematical decisions with and without mathematical probabilities are emphasized, and some resampling techniques such as the bootstrap are used to estimate variances of parameters in yield-mortality models described in Chapter 2. Bootstrapping is also used in a simple and direct approach to risk analysis and precautionary fishery management.

Contents

List of Figures

List of Tables

Glossary

Symbol	Meaning	Unit of measurement
a	Intercept of the length-weight relationship	---
A	Finite rate of total mortality	---
a_d	Compensation factor	---
ALIM	Fish for subsistence in the coastal zone	tonnes
area	Area swept per day	km²/day
AREA	Area occupied by the stock	km²
AVE	Average value of fishing effort	$/ue
AY	Average yield	tonnes/ue
b	Exponent of the length-weight relationship	---
b_β	Base run value for the β management criterion	---
B	Population biomass	tonnes
B_{BE}	Biomass at bioeconomic equilibrium	tonnes
B_0	Initial biomass	tonnes
BE	Bioeconomic equilibrium: $\pi(t) = 0$	$
Beq	Equilibrium biomass	tonnes
B_{max}	Maximum biomass	tonnes
B_{OPT}	Optimum biomass	tonnes
B_∞	Virgin biomass	tonnes
c	Unitary cost of fishing effort	$/ue
Cinc	Average incidental catch per fishing trip	tonnes
c_p	Processing costs	$/yr
CPUE	Catch per unit of effort	tonnes/ue
$CPUE_{max}$	Maximum observed catch per unit of effort	tonnes/ue
d	Discrete discount rate	---
$D_1, D_2,...D_\xi$	Alternative management strategies in decision analysis	---
D_{kh}	Distance from port h to fishing ground k	km
DAYS	Average number of fishing days per month	#
DEL_{HS}	Average time delay of egg maturation	months
DEL_m	Average time delay of vessels entry to the fishery	months
DT	Time increment	t
$E_\mu{}^*$	Optimum vector value of the multiple criteria function	---
$E_{\beta\mu}$	β criterion value of the management goal μ	---
E_μ	Vector of values for the multi-criteria function corresponding to the management option μ, assessed in time horizon (0,T)	---
EMP	Employment generated by the fishery	#
EV	Expected value of the NPV	$
EXP_m	Export earnings, harvesting sector	$
EXP_P	Export earnings, processing sector	$
f	Fishing effort	ue
f_{kl}	Fishing intensity exerted in site with geographic coordinates kl	days
fa	Cumulative spatial allocation of fishing intensity	---
f_{BE}	Fishing effort at bioeconomic equilibrium	ue
f_{MBP}	Fishing effort at maximum biological production	ue
f_{MEY}	Fishing effort at maximum economic yield	ue
f_{MSY}	Fishing effort at maximum sustainable yield	ue
f_{OPT}	Optimal effort	ue

F	Instantaneous rate of fishing mortality	1/t
F_{MBP}	Instantaneous fishing mortality at maximum biological production	1/t
F_{MEY}	Instantaneous fishing mortality at maximum economic yield	1/t
F_{MSY}	Instantaneous fishing mortality at maximum sustainable yield	1/t
FC	Daily fixed cost per vessel	$
FEC	Mean fecundity per female	# eggs
$FISH_m$	Mean number of fishermen per vessel type m	# ind
FR	Finite rate of fishing mortality	---
g	Delay order	---
$g_{\beta\phi}$	Target for the β criterion of the goal set ϕ in multi-criteria optimization	---
h	Port	---
H	Proportion of females	---
Hmax	Maximum annual number of eggs produced by the spawning stock	# eggs
HS	Number of eggs produced by the spawning stock	# eggs
i	Species	---
I	Indifference curve	---
ITG	Individual transferable ground	---
ITQ	Individual transferable quota	tonnes
j	Age	---
k	Locality coordinate: latitude; fishing ground	---
kp	Curvature parameter of the von Bertalanffy growth equation	1/t
K	Carrying capacity of the environment	tonnes
l	Locality coordinate: longitude	---
L	Individual length	mm
$L_{50\%}$	Length at 50 % gear retention	mm
$L_{75\%}$	Length at 75 % gear retention	mm
L_{∞}	Asymptotic length of the von Bertalanffy growth equation	mm
LLi	Lower limit of constants or variable functions in the "Complex" method	---
LOSS	Value of the loss matrix in decision theory	---
m	Type of vessel or fleet	---
M	Instantaneous rate of natural mortality	1/t
MAGE	Maximum age	t
MBP	Maximum biological production	tonnes
MEY	Maximum economic yield	tonnes
MR	Finite rate of natural mortality	---
MSY	Maximum sustainable yield	tonnes
MTPR	Marginal time preference rate	%
MVE	Marginal value of fishing effort	$/ue
MY	Marginal yield	tonnes/ue
N	Population abundance	# ind
NPV	Net present value	$
NT	Number of recruits in each patch (CHART model)	# ind
OVC	Other variable costs (bait, maintenance and repair, gear replacement)	$/yr
OSY	Optimum sustainable yield	tonnes
p	Average price of a species	$/tonne
pcap	Probability of capture	---
P_k	Probability of finding the target species in fishing ground k	---
P_{λ}	Probability of occurrence of an event λ	---

Pinc	Average price paid per ton of incidental catch	\$/tonne
Ptar	Average price paid for target species	\$/tonne
$PV\pi$	Present value of net revenues	\$
q	Catchability coefficient	---
qua	Catchability coefficient per unit area	---
quasi π	Quasi rent of variable costs	\$
Q	Fisher income	\$/t
r	Intrinsic rate of population growth	---
R_j	Estimated recruitment at age j	# ind
R_{kl}	Number of recruits located in the patch center of the cell kl	ind/t
$Risk_{kl}$	Perceived risk of fishing in ground kl	1 to 3
Rmax	Maximum observed recruitment	# ind
RET	Retention of fishing gear	%
RN	Random variable of recruitment equation	ind/t
RV	Random variable of catch equation	tonnes/t
s_i	Age at sexual maturity	t
S	Finite survival rate	---
S1, S2	Specific gear retention constants	---
SAE	A (0, 1) distribution of fishing effort	---
SEL	Selectivity of fishing gear	%
SG	Number of rows in a geographic grid	---
SN	States of nature	---
t	Time	d, mo, yr
t_c	Age at first capture	t
t_o	Hypothetical age at zero length (von Bertalanffy growth equation)	t
TC	Total costs	\$
TG	Number of columns in a geographic grid	#
TR	Total revenues	\$
TSR	Total sustainable revenues	\$
TSG	Cell length for a specific spatial resolution (degrees, minutes, seconds)	km
TTG	Cell width for a specific spatial resolution (degrees, minutes, seconds)	km
ue	Unit of effort	various
U	Catch per unit of effort (general notation)	tonnes/ue
ULi	Upper limit of constants or variable functions in the Complex method	---
v	Discount factor	---
V	Number of vessels	#
VAR	Variance of the expected NPV	\$
VC	Variable costs of fishing effort	\$
w_p	wholesale price	\$
W	Individual weight	g
W_∞	Asymptotic weight	g
x	Distance from the site kl to the center of the patch	km
xp	ex-vessel price	\$
Y	Yield	tonnes
Y_{MBP}	Yield at maximum biological production	tonnes
Y_{MEY}	Yield at maximum economic yield	tonnes
Z	Instantaneous rate of total mortality	1/t
Z_{MBP}	Instantaneous rate of total mortality at MBP	1/t
Z_{MEY}	Instantaneous rate of total mortality at MEY	1/t
Z_{MSY}	Instantaneous rate of total mortality at MSY	1/t

α_{XY}	Competition coefficient that measures the per capita effect of Y on X	---
α_{YX}	Competition coefficient that measures the per capita effect of X on Y	---
β	Criterion value with regard to a management option μ	---
β_1	Predation coefficient	---
β_2	Predation coefficient	---
δ	Continuous discount rate	---
ε	Proportion of the catch that goes to the export market	---
ϕ	Friction of distance	---
γ_g (t)	Output of the delay process (e.g. number of vessels entering the fishery along the season)	# / t
γ_1 (t)... γ_{g-1} (t)	Intermediate rates of the delay process	# / t
φ	Fleet dynamic parameter	---
λ	States of nature in decision theory	#
μ	Management option	---
π	Net revenues	$
πm	Marginal rent	$/ue
θ	Average cost of oil and gas per km traveled	$/km
σ	Standard deviation (0< σ < 1) of patch density	---
$\overline{\upsilon}\mu$	Decision parameter vector corresponding to a management option μ	---
$\upsilon\overline{\mu}^*$	Parameter vector for optimal control of the fishery	---
ϖ	Proportion assigned to the crew as labor payment	[0,1]
ξ	Management options in decision theory	#
$\Omega\beta\mu\phi$	Normalized deviation of the criterion β with respect to management option μ and goal set ϕ	---
Ψ	Total consumption	---

1. Inherent Characteristics of Fish Stocks

Fisheries management is a complex process that requires the integration of resource biology and ecology, with socio-economic and institutional factors affecting the behavior of fishers and policy makers. The purpose of this multidisciplinary field is to aid decision-making to achieve a sustainable development of the activity, so that future generations can also benefit from the resource. However, sustainability has been far more difficult to achieve that is commonly thought: fish populations are becoming increasingly limited, world catch has begun to drop, and almost 70% of the individual fish stocks around the world are fully to heavily exploited, overexploited or depleted (Garcia & Newton, 1997). Indeed, depressed yields, coupled with a rise in demand and prices, determined a systematic decreasing trend in catch rates and global landings. Conventional management measures, such as minimum size limits and reductions in catch or in fishing effort, have been used to promote stock rebuilding by reducing fishing mortality and increasing survival of spawning stocks. However, uncertainty levels in stock estimates, impressive and hidden changes in fishing power, coupled with a risk prone management attitude and a high inter temporal preference in resource use, have determined drastic collapses of some stocks, even under an "a priori" successful management scenario (Ludwig *et al.*, 1993). What are the reasons for management failure? How could this syndrome of overexploitation be explained? Among the multiple reasons that have been invoked to explain this, some inevitably arise from the inherent characteristics of both the fish stock and the fishery. To further understand management limitations of fish stocks, the following sections discuss the basic assumptions underlying the optimal allocation of natural resources, and the inherent characteristics of fisheries that prevent the market, under unrestricted access, from optimally allocating fishery resources. To mitigate these undesired effects, the bioeconomic literature invokes the allocation of property rights, which requires consideration of a management context. Thus, we provide some guidelines for developing fishery management plans.

1.1. Optimal allocation of renewable resources: basic assumptions

To have an optimal allocation of natural resources in a specific economy, non-attenuated property rights need to be specified. Those rights must be (Randall, 1981, Schmid, 1978):

Completely specified in terms of the rights that accompany the property over the resource, the restrictions over those rights, and the penalties corresponding to their violation.

Exclusive, so that the person who has those rights will also be responsible for any retributions and penalties corresponding to the use of the natural resource.

Transferable, in order to have those rights in the hands of those who have the capability to convey them to the highest use value.

Effectively enforced, because a non-policed right becomes an empty right.

1.2. The failure in the optimal allocation of fishery resources

In fisheries, the basic assumptions of the neoclassic market model mentioned above are violated. Thus, overexploitation, both biological and economic, has been a common feature of many important fisheries around the world. Fishery resources have special inherent characteristics that distinguish them from other natural renewable resources and that require further discussion in order to understand short and long-term exploitation patterns.

Property regimes, property rights and externalities

Fishery resources could be subjected to four different property regimes: state, private, common (*res communis*) and open access (*res nullius*). The relevant concepts analyzed by Bromley (1991) are used to characterize each regime, as follows:

- If resource users have the duty to observe rules and norms of use/access determined by a government institution that has the right of its management, then the fishery is state property.
- If the fishers have the right to decide on socially acceptable uses of the resource, even though they have the duty to abstain from destructive uses, the exploitation regime is deemed private property.
- If the State has allocated property rights to a well-defined group of fishers who have specific rights and duties with respect to the rates of resource use, then the exploitation regime is of common property (*res communis*). This situation implies a necessary but not sufficient condition for failure in the optimal allocation of a resource. This is because common property regimes consider exclusion of non-participant and specific duties to resource users, who cannot by themselves make decisions that lead to the collapse of the fishery. The efficiency of alternative management actions imposed by the management authority, and the clear specification of rights and duties for the owners, are critical to avoid fishery collapse.
- In open access (*res nullius*) conditions, the resource as property does not exist, and thus any member of society could harvest the resource. This regime fails to lead to optimal resource allocation, and thus constitutes a sufficient condition for resource overexploitation (Anderson, 1977; Hannesson, 1978). Two situations arise: (1) unrestricted access to the resource and (2) generation of externalities between resource users.

Externalities

Externalities are defined as every external effect caused by individual fishers but not included in their accounting system. Fishing externalities are commonly negative and occur when fishers can freely enter and capture a resource, and where a voluntary agreement of co-operation does not exist; in these cases, resource users do not consider the external effects impose on others. Three types of negative externalities have been identified in most fisheries (Smith, 1969; Agnello & Donnelley, 1976): associated with the stock, crowding, and fishing gear. Before we extend this classification to account for other type of externalities, including positive ones, these three can be specified as follows:

Stock externalities. These occur when entry of new vessels reduces stock availability and hence the harvesting costs of others. Fishers do not consider these costs because they only take into account their private fishing trip costs (internal); ignoring the external costs imposed to others by stock reduction.

Crowding externalities. These arise when vessel aggregation on the fishing grounds increases marginal catch costs. Occurrence of such externalities depends on the extension of the fishing ground and the stock magnitude. Fishing effort will not be perfectly allocated in space (*e.g.*, over the greatest resource concentrations) and time (*e.g.*, they would wait to have access to a limited fishing ground). This externality is commonly seen in sedentary species with patchy distribution, where the exploiting strategy tends to sequentially deplete the most profitable beds.

Technological externalities. Arise when the fishing gear changes the population structure, dynamics of the target species and associated bycatch, imposing negative effects to other fishers, and affecting the abundance of incidental species which might constitute the target of other fisheries. Two types of technological externalities could be distinguished:

(iii.1) Sequential externalities. Occur when artisanal and industrial fleets exploit different components of the population structure of the same species, thus affecting each other. Artisanal vessels tend to apply their fishing effort close to the coastal zone where juveniles inhabit, while the industrial fleet generally operates in deeper waters, exploiting the adult component of a stock. Thus, a substantial increase in fishing effort of the artisanal fleet would cause recruitment overfishing and a decrease in stock availability for the industrial fleet in subsequent periods, *i.e.*, a negative externality for the industrial fleet. Analogously, an increase in fishing effort of the industrial fleet will diminish the spawning stock, affecting subsequent recruitment and thus stock availability for the artisanal fleet.

(iii.2) Incidental externalities. These arise in technological interdependent fisheries, when fleets use non-discriminatory fishing gears, *e.g.*, a bycatch in fishery *A* diminishes the abundance of those species that constitute the target for fishery *B*. The non-accounted negative external effect for fishers belonging to fishery *A* constitutes an incidental externality. It is commonly observed in shrimp and demersal fisheries, where the shrimp fishery generates incidental catches of demersal species, a non-accounted negative effect that generates an externality to the demersal fishing fleet.

Ecologically based externalities. Suppose that two competing species constitute the target of different fisheries; variations in fishing intensity exerted by both fleets would change the magnitude and direction of the ecological interaction and thus the relative abundance of both species. Consider two fisheries *A* and *B* that capture, respectively, the competing species S_1 and S_2, which coexist without exploitation. An increase in fishing effort over species S_1 will determine an increment in abundance of species S_2, exploited by fishery *B*. Thus, fishery *A* generates an external positive effect to fishery *B*, defined as an externality under competitive coexistence.

Alternatively, suppose that without human impact, the competitively subordinate species S_2 is excluded by the dominant S_1. Fishing effort exerted by fishery *A* will diminish S_1, determining an increment of S_2, harvested by fishery *B*, due to an increasing availability of a limited resource (*e.g.* space, food). Thus, fishery *A* generates an external positive effect to fishery *B*, which constitutes an externality by competitive release.

A predator-prey interdependence can also guide the direction of the externality. Consider a simple situation of a predator-prey relationship that can be modelled by the Lotka-Volterra equilibrium equations. An increase in fishing effort of fishery *A*, which has prey S_p as the target, will generate a decrease in the abundance of predator S_d, harvested by fishery *B* (consider a specialist predator *sensu* Begon *et al.*, 1990), causing a negative externality. Analogously, when fishing effort is increased in fishery *B*, prey abundance increases, generating a positive externality to fishery *A*. Both external effects constitute a trophic-based externality.

Techno-ecological externalities. These occur when e.g., a fishing gear disturbs the habitat of the target and other co-occurring species that might constitute the target for other fisheries. These externalities are common in benthic stocks harvested with trawls. For example, destruction of the benthic biogenic habitat could diminish the probability of recolonization and recruitment (Botsford *et al.*, 1997). The quality of the fishing ground (*e.g.*, available space for settlement, food availability) could mitigate the effect of the externality.

High exclusion costs

Inherent characteristics of fish stocks generate high costs of excluding other fishers from exploiting the resource. The open access regime, combined with high uncertainty levels in stock magnitude, determines that a fisher may not benefit by postponing a catch with the expectation of catching a larger and probably more valuable fish later, since that fish is likely to be caught in the meantime by another fisher. In other words, a single fisher cannot affect the size of the stock by reducing his catch rate, unless all or most other fishers agree to abstain proportionately (Eckert, 1979). Consequently, each fisher will increase his catch rate, and thus will generate high exclusion costs. Traditional schemes oriented to avoid high exclusion costs involve strategic institutional structures (*e.g.* property rights-based approaches, co-management schemes) and operational sets of management measures (*sensu* Charles, 1995; see also Orensanz & Jamieson, 1998). At least 4 approaches could be recognized: (i) resource privatization through the allocation of individual quotas; (ii) state intervention through the regulation of size and composition of the catch and the intensity of fishing effort; (iii) implementation of community-based management systems (Berkes, 1985, 1989; Smith & Berkes, 1991); or (iv) mixed strategies based on a combination of the above schemes (Defeo, 1993a, b; Seijo, 1993; Castilla, 1994; Castilla *et al.*, 1998).

Social trap in fisheries, and the free rider behavior

Without an agreement to limit catches, the main result of a single fisher's reduced catch rate is to lower the extraction cost of other fisher without necessarily increasing his benefits. Consequently, each fisher will increase the catch rate and thus contribute to destroy the fishery, an undesired long-run result for all fishers involved. Using Schelling's (1978) terminology, this constitutes a social trap in fisheries because the micro-motives of an individual fisher in the short-run are not consistent and compatible with the macro-results that he and the other fishers desire in the long run. The short-run fishers micro-motives consist in catching as many fish as possible in order to increase their marginal benefits, while the long-run desired macro-results may involve achieving the maximum sustainable yield. Uncertainty of future stock availability determines that long-run results are usually dominated by marginal benefits in the short-run. The sustainable yield of a fishery, given certain intertemporal preferences of resource use, will be an attainable goal only when the number of fishers is limited by some kind of effort regulation and act in concert.

The size of the group of fishers is a relevant factor affecting the avoidance of this social trap. If the group is large, a fisher may be an unintentional free rider or non-contributing user when he cannot avoid the macro-result (fishery collapse) because he cannot be sure that the behavior of other fishers will sustain resource yield. This kind of user is usually found when there is not a voluntary collective action by most community members to prevent resource depletion, and also when uncertainty exists about stock abundance (which is the usual case). When the group is small, exclusion costs are not necessarily lower, but the non-contributing user could be easily identified, therefore reducing the number of free riders (Schmid, 1987).

High transaction costs

Marine fisheries involved high transaction costs, which also attenuate an efficient allocation of fisheries resources over time. Transaction costs involve information costs, enforcement or policing costs and contractual costs (Schmid, 1987, Randall, 1981).

Information costs. Fisheries management implies high information costs resulting from interdisciplinary research efforts in biology, ecology, statistics and socio-economics. This research is needed to keep track of: (1) fish population dynamics and stock magnitude; (2) environmental variability; (3) spatial dynamics of catches and fishing effort; (4) changes in intertemporal preferences of the society as a result of fluctuations in market demand and resource availability. Overall increase in fishing are usually not accompanied by a corresponding increase in scientific and fishery information, which in turn led to poor management and overfishing, increase of harvesting costs and the consequent reduction of the economic rent of the fishery. This situation becomes even more complex with the large uncertainties observed in natural systems, as well as in biological, social, political and economic factors (Hilborn & Peterman, 1996), thus increasing the probability of having non-contributing users, stock depletion and economic rent dissipation.

Enforcement costs. Fisheries management involves high enforcement or policing costs resulting from the implementation of management schemes and allocation of property rights. In many cases, policing areas are so extensive (oceanic fisheries) or accessible to third parties (*e.g.* recreational harvesters in hand-gathering intertidal stocks and harvesting infralittoral stocks by scuba) that policing effort is extensive and ineffective. When this happens, the non-enforceable right becomes an empty right. The above-mentioned aspects, coupled with low operating costs, caused the collapse of many coastal fisheries (Defeo *et al.*, 1993).

Contractual costs. This type of transaction costs occurs in countries where there have been legislative efforts directed to promote collective forms of organizations (*e.g.* cooperatives), giving them exploitation rights over certain resources. In this context, costs directed to foster this kind of organizations are usually substantial, so it is necessary to identify who (*e.g.* fishers or State) will pay for the contractual costs. Something similar happens when the State is interested in promoting a certain management strategy, as the implementation of Individual Transferable Quotas (*ITQ*: Geen & Nayar, 1988) or Individual Transferable Grounds (*ITG*: Seijo, 1993) between the members of a fishery community in order to maximize resource rent over time.

After recognizing the inherent characteristics of fishery resources, which provide the major elements of the management context, the next section summarizes the main steps needed to develop intelligent management plans.

1.3. Fisheries management plans

The intertemporal flow of costs and benefits of alternative management strategies should be sustained by a robust analysis of the fishery as a whole. For this purpose, static and dynamic bioeconomic models constitute an important aid to decision-making aiming at a sustainable management of fish stocks. The necessary steps for fisheries management planning can be summarized as follows (Seijo *et al.*, 1991a):

- Evaluate the fishery in a biological, ecological and economic sense. The size and dynamics of the stock, fleet(s) and catches, the temporary flows of costs and benefits, direct and indirect employment and generated incomes, as well as critical environmental variables that could be used to explain fluctuations in stock distribution and abundance, must be carefully analyzed.

- Identify and quantify the objectives and goals of management.

- Select the appropriate combination of performance variables, both biological and economic, and determine the control variables that allow achieving the desired levels in fishery performance criteria.

- Determine alternative management strategies and their mechanisms of implementation, in order to make operative the control variables previously defined. To select an adequate management vector, it is useful to explore the dynamic behavior of the fishery by using mathematical models that incorporate the main elements of the system. For this purpose:

    (a) carefully specify the fishery system and the context in which the model is intended to operate;
    (b) elaborate a causal diagram with the recognized fishery subsystems and the corresponding interface variables;
    (c) build a block diagram to quantitatively define model subsystems and interactions among them, as well as exogenous and policy variables and their impact upon the system.

- Monitor the fishery to evaluate the impacts of alternative management strategies included in the management plan. Determine if the objectives and management goals are being achieved, and identify those factors that could preclude their consecution. Some hypotheses could be stated upon the simulation model already built in order to estimate the impact of alternative regulatory schemes.

- Reevaluate periodically the fishery, the objectives and established management goals.

1.4. A closing comment

The bioeconomic literature invokes the allocation of property rights as a way to mitigate the undesired effects caused by the inherent characteristics of fisheries, and thus to attenuate the risks of stock overexploitation. In this context, the bioeconomic impacts resulting from alternative management strategies must be evaluated, as well as the adequate policy instruments that should be used to satisfy biological and economic criteria. These include biomass levels, yields, net revenues, direct employment, export earnings and contribution to the alimentary production of the region. For this purpose, static and dynamic bioeconomic models have been developed as a theoretical framework for the design of intelligent management schemes aiming at sustainable use of fish stocks. The remaining chapters of the book will address these topics.

2. Bioeconomic Models

In order to perform estimations and predictions of the bioeconomic impact derived from different management strategies, a dynamic modelling approach of the resource and the fishery as a whole is needed. In this Section we develop: (1) the static and dynamic versions of the Gordon-Schaefer (Gordon, 1953, 1954) model; (2) a distributed-delays fleet dynamics model based on Smith's (1969) model; (3) yield-mortality models; and (4) age-structured dynamic models (Seijo & Defeo, 1994a).

2.1. The Gordon-Schaefer model

The logistic equation (Verhulst, 1838) describes population growth based on the following mathematical expression (Graham, 1935):

$$\frac{dB}{dt} = rB(t)(1 - \frac{B(t)}{K}) \quad \textbf{(2.1)}$$

where r is the intrinsic rate of population growth, $B(t)$ is population biomass in time t and K is the carrying capacity of the environment. Population behavior through time is described as a sigmoid curve, where the unexploited biomass increases until a maximum level $B\infty$, constrained by K (Fig. 2.1: see Pella & Tomlinson, 1969; Schaefer, 1954 for details).

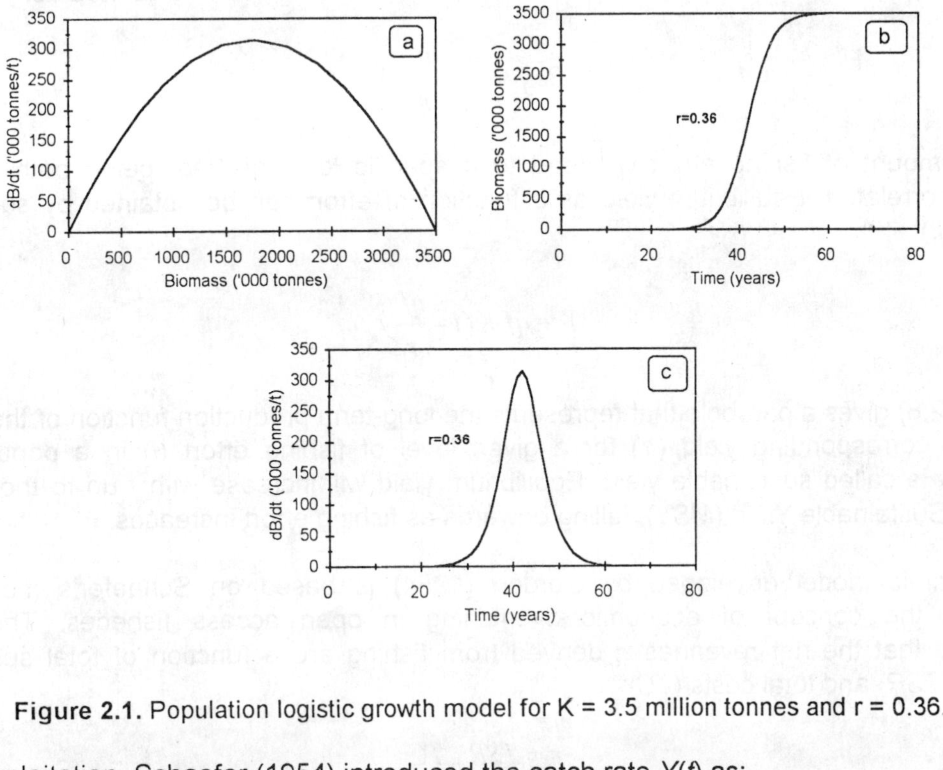

Figure 2.1. Population logistic growth model for K = 3.5 million tonnes and r = 0.36.

Under exploitation, Schaefer (1954) introduced the catch rate $Y(t)$ as:

$$Y(t) = q\,f(t)B(t) \tag{2.2}$$

where *f(t)* is the fishing effort and *q* is the catchability coefficient, defined as the fraction of the population fished by an effort unit (Gulland, 1983). Biomass changes through time can be expressed as:

$$\frac{dB}{dt} = rB[1 - \frac{B}{K}] - Y \tag{2.3}$$

When the population is at equilibrium, *i.e., dB/dt* =0, and thus losses by natural and fishing mortalities are compensated by the population increase due to individual growth and recruitment. Equilibrium yield can be defined as:

$$Y = rB(1 - \frac{B}{K}) \tag{2.4}$$

$$\frac{Y}{rB} + \frac{B}{K} = 1 \tag{2.5}$$

Substituting (2.2) in (2.5):

$$\frac{qfB}{rB} + \frac{B}{K} = 1 \tag{2.6}$$

Thus, the equilibrium biomass (*Beq*) as a function of fishing effort can be defined as:

$$Beq = (1 - \frac{qf}{r})K \tag{2.7}$$

A given amount of fishing effort will lead to a specific level of *Beq*, being both variables inversely correlated. Equilibrium yield as a function of effort can be obtained by substituting (2.7) in (2.2):

$$Y = qf\,K(1 - \frac{qf}{r}) \tag{2.8}$$

Equation (2.8) gives a parabola that represents the long-term production function of the fishery, where the corresponding yield (*Y*) for a given level of fishing effort (*f*) in a population at equilibrium is called sustainable yield. Equilibrium yield will increase with *f* up to the point of Maximum Sustainable Yield (*MSY*), falling onwards as fishing effort increases.

The economic model developed by Gordon (1954) is based on Schaefer's model, and introduced the concept of economic overfishing in open access fisheries. The model establishes that the net revenues π derived from fishing are a function of total sustainable revenues (*TSR*) and total costs (*TC*):

$$\pi = TSR - TC \tag{2.9}$$

or, alternatively:

$$\pi = pY - cf \tag{2.10}$$

where *p* is the (constant) price of the species and *c* the (constant) costs per unit of effort. The latter includes fixed costs, variable costs and opportunity costs of labor and capital. Fixed costs are independent of fishing operations (depreciation, administration and insurance costs), whereas variable costs are incurred when fishers go fishing (fuel, bait, food and beverages, etc.). Opportunity costs are the net benefits that could have been achieved in the next best economic activity, *i.e.*, other regional fisheries, capital investment or alternative employment, and thus must be integrated in cost estimations.

Substituting (2.2) in (2.10), π can be defined as a function of effort:

$$\pi = [\,pqB - c\,]f \tag{2.11}$$

As in the biological model, Gordon (1954) assumes equilibrium to obtain the long-term production function of the fishery. The open-access equilibrium yield occurs when *TSR* equals *TC* and thus $\pi(t) = 0$, and there will be no stimulus for entry or exit to the fishery. If, additionally, biomass is assumed at equilibrium, the yield thus established will provide a simultaneous equilibrium in both an economic and a biological sense, leading to *bioeconomic equilibrium (BE)*. Biomass at bioeconomic equilibrium (B_{BE}) can be defined by solving equation (2.11) for *B*:

$$B_{BE} = \frac{c}{qp} \tag{2.12}$$

B(t) will be always greater than 0, because fishing effort will be reduced or even ceased at *TC* ≥ *TSR*. Thus, the model predicts: (1) *overexploitation*, if the *TC* curve intersects the *TSR* curve at higher effort levels than those required to operate at *MSY*; and (2) *non-extinction of the resource*, because at effort levels above *BE* there will be no stimulus to entry to the fishery. The non-extinction prediction will depend on the rate of growth of the stock and the form of the function defined by equation 2.2 (Clark, 1985; Anderson, 1986). It will be correct if and only if the resulting biomass at *BE* exceeds a threshold biomass level required for a population to be viable.

TSR at equilibrium can be obtained by multiplying (2.4) by the unit price *p*:

$$TSR = prB\left[1 - \frac{B}{K}\right] \tag{2.13}$$

The *TSR* curve as a function of effort will have the same form as the sustainable yield curve, but in monetary terms (Fig. 2.1c). *TC* is obtained from equation (2.2), as a function of fishing effort:

$$qfB = rB\left[1 - \frac{B}{K}\right] \tag{2.14}$$

The long-term function of *TC* is calculated by solving for *f* and multiplying by *c*:

$$TC = \frac{cr[1-(B/K)]}{q} \tag{2.15}$$

Hence, the long-run sustainable biomass and production functions of the fishery can be built by specifying the corresponding levels of fishing effort at Maximum Economic Yield (f_{MEY}), Maximum Sustai·‧ble Yield (f_{MSY}) and bioeconomic equilibrium (f_{BE}) (Fig. 2.2).

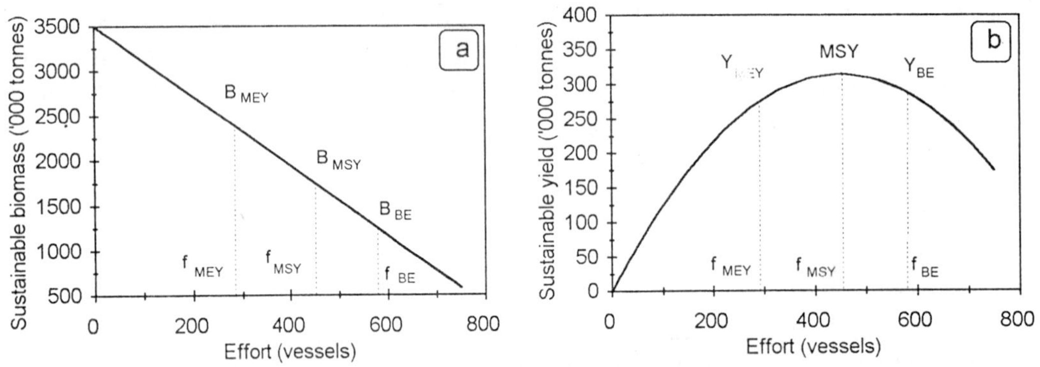

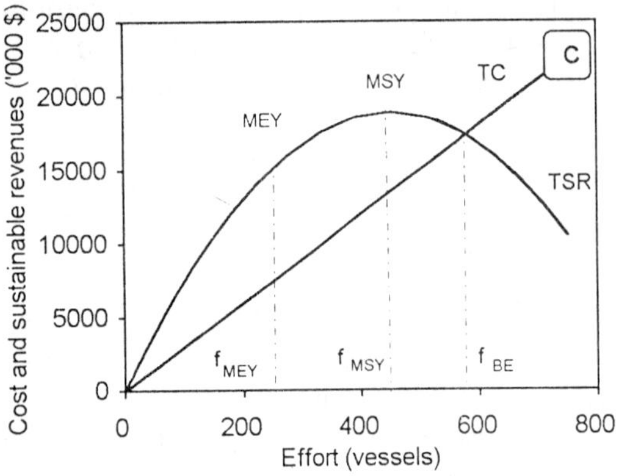

Figure 2.2. Gordon-Schaefer static model. Sustainable (a) biomass, (b) yield, and (c) total sustainable revenues (*TSR*) and costs (*TC*).

Under unrestricted access, the net benefit or economic rent of the fishery is positive when $f < f_{BE}$, and zero when *TC* equals *TSR* (Fig. 2.2c). The area under the *TSR* curve and above *TC* corresponds to the economic rent, which is maximized at *MEY* and the corresponding f_{MEY}, where the difference between *TC* and *TSR* is highest. The position of the *TC* curve will determine changes in *MEY* and *BE* levels. It is assumed that additional effort is produced by the entry of additional fishing units, instead of effort expansion by the already existing vessels (Anderson, 1986). Gordon (1954) predicts that f_{BE} will be twice f_{MEY} (see below).

Marginal and average yields

Both average (*AY*) and marginal (*MY*) yields correspond to the application of an additional unit of effort, and will be sustainable per unit of time. The former continuously falls as effort increases (Fig. 2.3a), until reaching 0 when the resource is exhausted. *MY* decreases more sharply than *AY* and reaches 0 at *MSY*, beyond which it takes negative values, *i.e.*, the yield obtained by an additional effort unit is progressively lower than the preceding one. This happens because each fisher operates according to variations in his AY, and does not take into account the external effects caused to other users and to the fishery as a whole.

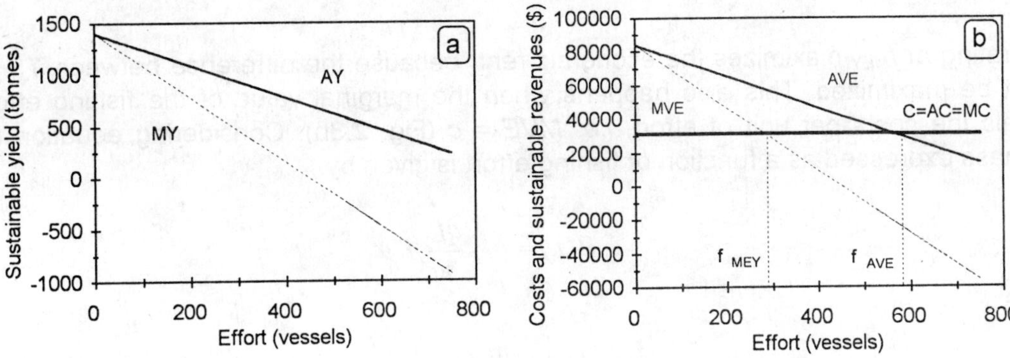

Figure 2.3. Open access regime. (a) Sustainable average and marginal yields; (b) average and marginal costs, and revenues, as a function of effort under open access conditions.

Effort levels at *MSY*, *MEY* and *BE*

One biological goal is to set effort and yield levels at MSY through time. For this end, we can take the first derivative of the yield function in (2.8):

$$\frac{dY}{df} = qK - \frac{2q^2 fK}{r} = 0 \qquad \textbf{(2.16)}$$

Solving for f and rearranging, the effort level at MSY is obtained as:

$$\frac{2q^2 fK}{r} = qK \qquad \textbf{(2.17)}$$

Thus:

$$f = \frac{qKr}{2q^2K} \qquad \textbf{(2.18)}$$

$$f_{MSY} = \frac{r}{2q} \qquad \textbf{(2.19)}$$

MSY is calculated by substituting (2.19) in (2.8):

$$Y = \frac{qKr}{2q} - \frac{q^2Kr^2}{4q^2r} \qquad \textbf{(2.20)}$$

and:

$$Y = \frac{Kr}{2} - \frac{Kr}{4}$$

So:

$$Y_{MSY} = \frac{Kr}{4} \tag{2.21}$$

Operating at f_{MEY} maximizes the economic rent, because the difference between *TSR* and *TC* must be maximized. This also happens when the marginal value of the fishing effort (*MVE*) equals the costs per unit of effort, *i.e.* $MVE = c$ (Fig. 2.3b). Considering equation (2.2), the biomass expressed as a function of fishing effort is given by:

$$B(t) = (1 - \frac{qf}{r})K$$

Thus:

$$Y(t) = qfK(1 - \frac{qf}{r}) \tag{2.22}$$

Multiplying (2.22) by the average price of the species and dividing by *f*, the average value of the fishing effort (*AVE*) is obtained:

$$AVE = qKp(1 - \frac{qf}{r}) \tag{2.23}$$

Solving equation (2.8) for *f*:

$$\frac{dY}{df} = qK(1 - \frac{2qf}{r})$$

The marginal value of fishing effort (*MVE*) is obtained by multiplying (2.23) by the average price of the species (*p*):

$$MVE = pqK(1 - \frac{2qf}{r}) \tag{2.24}$$

Fishing effort at *MEY* (f_{MEY}) is obtained by equaling (2.24) to the unit cost of fishing effort (*c*), and solving for *f*:

$$f_{MEY} = \frac{r}{2q}(1 - \frac{c}{pqK}) \tag{2.25}$$

The bioeconomic equilibrium is reached when *AVE* equals the costs per unit of effort ($AVE = c$: Fig. 2.3b). The latter can be estimated by equaling (2.23) to costs (*c*) and solving for *f*. It will be noted that $f_{BE} = 2f_{MEY}$, *i.e.*, f_{BE} is twice f_{MEY}.

Model assumptions

The economic model developed by Gordon also takes into account the assumptions considered by Schaefer (1954) for the biological model:

a) The population is at equilibrium (see above). Thus, it behaves in a more or less regular fashion such that changes in the trajectory of catch and effort could be used to reflect assertions about the future behavior of the system (Caddy, 1996).

b) Under equilibrium, fishing mortality (F) is proportional to effort (f), being the catchability coefficient (q) the constant of proportionality, *i.e.*:

$$F = qf \tag{2.26}$$

c) The catch per unit of effort (*CPUE*) is a relative index of population abundance:

$$CPUE = \frac{Y}{f} = qB \tag{2.27}$$

d) The stock is constrained by a constant carrying capacity of the environment.

e) The stock will respond immediately to variations in the magnitude of effort exerted.

f) Fishing technology is constant.

g) Prices and marginal/average costs are constant and independent of the level of effort exerted.

h) *TC* are proportional to effort, and thus a change in the slope of the *TC* curve will determine changes in *BE* and *MEY* levels.

Limitations

(a) All processes affecting stock productivity (*e.g.*, growth, mortality, and recruitment) are subsumed in the effective relationship between effort and catch.

(b) The catchability coefficient q is not always constant, and may differ due to e.g. different aggregation behavior of pelagic and sedentary resources. Factors related to differential gear selectivity by age/lengths are not taken into account.

(c) *CPUE* is not always an unbiased index of abundance. This is especially relevant for sedentary resources with patchy distribution and without the capacity of redistribution in the fishing ground once fishing effort is exerted. Sequential depletion of patches also determines a patchy distribution of resource users, precluding model applicability (see Caddy, 1975, 1989a, b; Conan, 1984; Orensanz *et al.*, 1991).

(d) Variations in the spatial distribution of the stock are usually ignored, as well as the biological processes that generate biomass, the intra/interspecific interactions, and stochastic fluctuations in the environment and in population abundance.

(e) Ecological and technological interdependencies (see Chapter 3) and differential allocation of fishing effort in the short term (see Chapter 6) are not usually taken into account.

(f) Improvement in technology and fishing power determines that q often varies through time.

(g) It becomes difficult to distinguish whether population fluctuations are due to fishing pressure or natural processes. In some fisheries, fishing effort could be exerted at levels greater than twice the optimum (Clark, 1985).

2.2. Fleet dynamics: a distributed-delay Smith's model

Smith (1969) assumes that long-run fishing effort levels are proportional to profits:

$$\frac{df}{dt} = \varphi\pi(t) \tag{2.28}$$

where φ is a positive constant that describes fleet dynamics in the *long-run* (short-run decisions are not considered). Changes in fishing effort are obtained by substituting (2.11) in (2.28):

$$\frac{df}{dt} = \varphi[\,pqB(t) - c\,]f(t) \tag{2.29}$$

Biomass changes through time are given by:

$$\frac{dB}{dt} = rB(t)[1 - \frac{B(t)}{K}] - qB(t)f \tag{2.30}$$

If $\pi(t) > 0$, vessels will enter the fishery; exit is expected to occur if $\pi(t) < 0$. Parameter φ can be empirically estimated according to variations in $\pi(t)$, which in turn will have a close relation with the incurred costs for different effort levels (Seijo *et al.*, 1994b).

Variations in fishing effort might not be reflected immediately in stock abundance and perceived yields. For this reason, Seijo (1987) improved Smith's model by incorporating the delay process between the moment fishers face positive or negative net revenues and the moment which entry or exit takes place. This is expressed by a distributed-delay parameter (*DEL*) represented by an Erlang probability density function (Manetsch, 1976), which describes the average time lag of vessel entry/exit to the fishery once the effect of changes in the net revenues is manifested (see also Chapter 6). Hence, the long-run dynamics of vessel type *m* ($V_m(t)$) can be described by a distributed delay function of order *g* by the following set of differential equations:

$$\tag{2.31}$$

$$\frac{d\gamma t_1}{dt} = \frac{g}{DEL_m}(V_m(t) - \gamma t_1(t))$$

$$\frac{d\gamma t_2}{dt} = \frac{g}{DEL_m}(\gamma t_1(t) - \gamma t_2(t))$$

$$\frac{d\gamma t_g}{dt} = \frac{g}{DEL_m}(\gamma t_{g-1} - \gamma t_g(t))$$

where V_m is the input to the delay process (number of vessels which will allocate their fishing effort to target species); $\gamma t_g(t)$ is the output of the delay process (number of vessels entering the fishery); $\gamma_1(t)$, $\gamma_2(t)$,..., $\gamma_{g-1}(t)$ are intermediate rates of the delay; DEL_m is the expected time of entry of vessels to the fishery; and *g* is the order of the delay. The parameter *g* specifies the member of the Gamma family of probability density functions.

Example 2.1. Dynamic bioeconomic model

Consider a pelagic fishery with parameters defined in Table 2.1.

Table 2.1. Parameters for the dynamic bioeconomic model (Gordon-Schaefer).

Parameter/Variable	Value
Intrinsic growth rate	0.36
Catchability coefficient	0.0004
Carrying capacity of the system	3500000 tonnes
Price of the target species	60 US$/tonne
Unit cost of fishing effort	30000 US$/yr
Initial population biomass	3500000 tonnes
Fleet dynamics parameter	0.000005

Fig. 2.4 shows variations in biomass, yield, costs and revenues resulting from the application of the dynamic and static versions of the Gordon-Schaefer model, as a function of different effort levels. f_{BE} is reached at 578 vessels and f_{MEY} at 289 vessels.

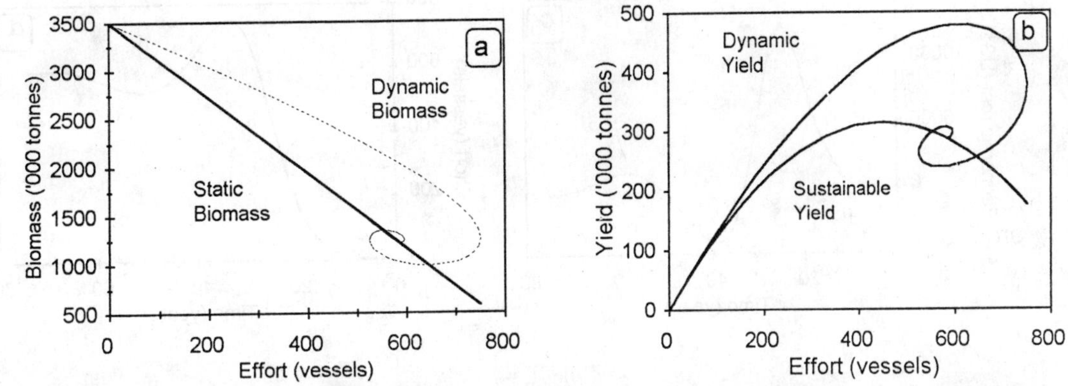

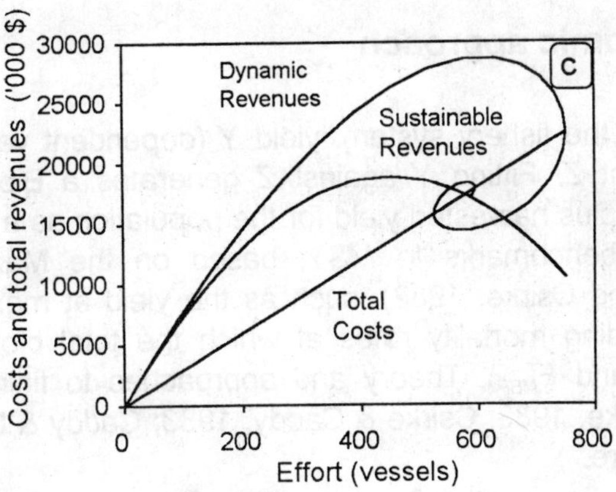

Figure 2.4. Static (equilibrium) and dynamic trajectories of biomass (a), yield (b) and cost-revenues (c) resulting from the application of different fishing effort levels.

Fig. 2.5 shows temporal fluctuations in performance variables of the fishery. Yield and net revenues decrease at fishing effort levels higher than 630 vessels, followed by a dynamic entry/exit of vessels to the fishery, as the economic rent becomes positive or negative, respectively. Bioeconomic equilibrium ($\pi = 0$) is reached at 1200 tonnes, after 50 years of fishing operations.

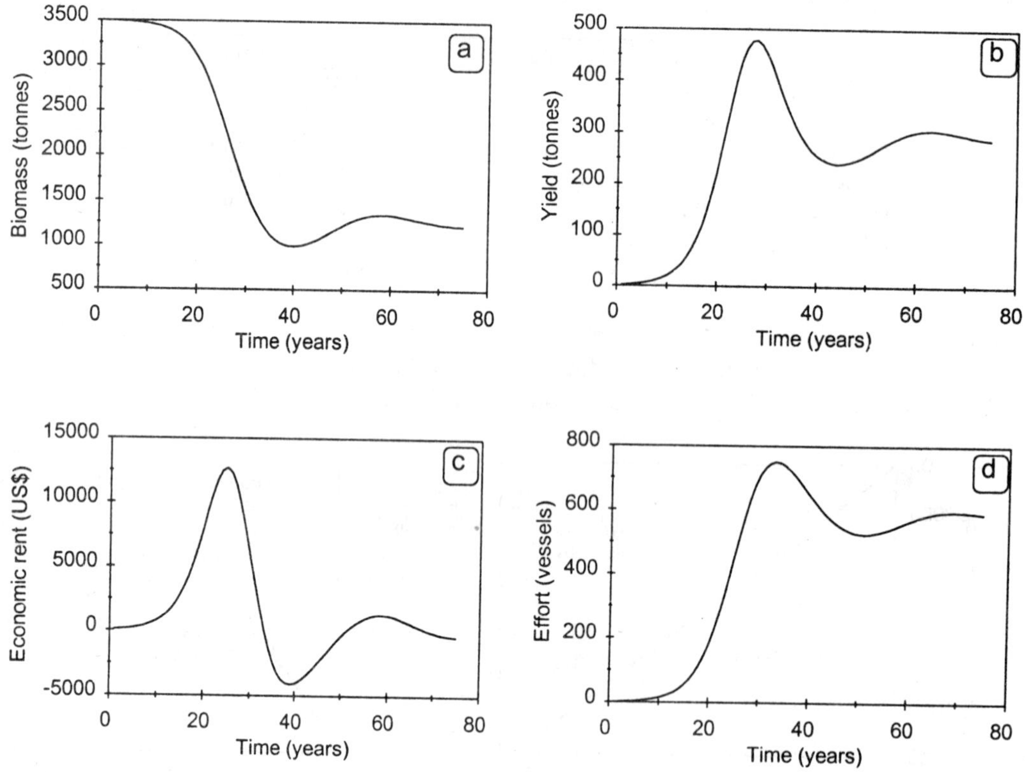

Figure 2.5. Dynamic trajectories of (a) biomass, (b) yield, (c) economic rent, and (d) fishing effort.

2.3. Yield-mortality models: a bioeconomic approach

Yield-mortality models link two main outputs of the fishery system: yield *Y* (dependent variable) and the instantaneous total mortality coefficient *Z*. Fitting *Y* against *Z* generates a Biological Production curve, which includes natural deaths plus harvested yield for the population as a whole (Figure 2.6). *Y-Z* models provide alternative benchmarks to *MSY*, based on the Maximum Biological Production (*MBP*) concept (Caddy and Csirke, 1983), such as the yield at maximum biological production (Y_{MBP}) and the corresponding mortality rates at which the total biological production of the system is maximised (Z_{MBP} and F_{MBP}). Theory and approaches to fitting the models have been fully described (Caddy & Csirke, 1983; Csirke & Caddy, 1983; Caddy & Defeo, 1996) and thus will not be considered in detail here.

Logistic model

Csirke & Caddy (1983) expressed the equilibrium yield equation of Graham (1935) in terms of the equilibrium value of annual mortality rate (see p. 45 and also Caddy, 1986), thus reducing equation (2.1) to a quadratic form:

$$Y_i = aZ_i^2 + bZ_i + c \qquad (2.32)$$

where Y_i and Z_i are the yield and the mean total mortality coefficient for year *i*, respectively.

Under logistic assumptions, equation (2.32) gives a parabola passing through the abscissa to the right of the origin. Using multiple regression, where Z_i and Z_i^2 are treated as two independent variables, the "convex-downwards" curve that relates annual values of yield and total mortality can be drawn. An estimate of the natural mortality coefficient *M* can be obtained by solving this equation for $Z = M$ (Y_i and $F = 0$). See Csirke & Caddy (1983) and Caddy & Defeo (1996) for the calculation of this and the other parameters related to the Biological Production curve (Fig. 2.5).

Csirke & Caddy (1983) suggested an alternative approach to fitting the logistic model, based on the abundance index:

$$_i = \frac{Y_i}{(Z_i - M)} \qquad (2.33)$$

which was fitted against $(Z_i\text{-}M)$, so that:

$$\frac{Y_i}{Z_i - M} = a - b(Z_i - M) \qquad (2.34)$$

The above equation was preferred owing to theoretical objections to the direct fitting procedure (Hoenig & Hoenig, 1986; Caddy & Defeo, 1996). This model is fitted by using different trial values of *M*, in which the best value selected is that which maximize a goodness of fit criterion (Caddy, 1986). Parameters of this logistic model can be obtained as in Caddy & Defeo (1996).

Exponential model

Caddy & Defeo (1996) extended the theory of production modelling with mortality estimates to include the exponential model of Fox (1970). Linear and non-linear approaches were used to fit this model. The exponential model for yield and mortality data can be summarized as:

$$\frac{Y_i}{Z_i - M} = B_\infty e^{-b'(Z_i - M)} \qquad (2.35)$$

where $B\infty$ and *b'* can be estimated by nonlinear regression techniques. As in the case of the alternative logistic approach, the model is fitted for different trial values of *M*, selecting those that maximize a goodness of fit criterion. The estimation procedure for the remaining parameters is fully explained in Caddy & Defeo (1996). A linearised approach of the above equation can be easily derived as:

$$\ln\left(\frac{Y_i}{Z_i - M}\right) = [\ln B\infty + b'M] - b' Z_i \qquad \textbf{(2.36)}$$

using $\ln(Y_i/Z_i - M)$ and Z_i as dependent and independent variables, respectively. Parameter estimation follows the same reasoning as in the previous approach, using trial values of M.

A precautionary bioeconomic approach

In order to obtain bioeconomic reference points (*RPs*) for precautionary fishery management (Caddy & Mahon, 1995), Defeo & Seijo (in press) developed an expression for the economic rent (π) of a stock from the exponential version of the yield-mortality model in its linearised form:

$$\pi = pF\, B_\infty e^{(-b'F)} - \frac{cF}{q} \qquad \textbf{(2.37)}$$

where p is the average price of the target species and c is the unitary cost of the fishing effort.

Differentiating the above equation, an expression that yields the marginal rent (πm) with changes in F is obtained:

$$\pi m(F) = \frac{d}{dF}\left(pFB_\infty\, e^{(b'F)} - c\frac{F}{q}\right) \qquad \textbf{(2.38)}$$

and:

$$\pi m(F) = pB_\infty\, e^{(b'F)} - pFB_\infty\, e^{(b'F)} - \frac{c}{q} \qquad \textbf{(2.39)}$$

Solving for F, an expression that provides the fishing mortality rate at *MEY* (F_{MEY}) is estimated as:

$$pB_\infty\, e^{(-b'F)} - pFB_\infty b' e^{(-b'F)} - \frac{c}{q} = 0 \qquad \textbf{(2.40)}$$

$$F_{MEY} = \frac{\left[-W\left[\frac{e^1}{pqB\infty}c\right] + 1\right]}{b'} \qquad \textbf{(2.41)}$$

By doing $a = \frac{e^1}{(pB_\infty q)}c$, a special function of MathCad ®[1] called $W[a]$ can be built as follows:

$$a = We^W \qquad \textbf{(2.42)}$$

F_{MEY} is calculated as:

$$F_{MEY} = \frac{-W + 1}{b'} \qquad \textbf{(2.43)}$$

Yield at *MEY* is given by:

---

[1] Mathcad 5.0 for Windows. 1994. Mathsoft, Inc.

$$Y_{MEY} = F_{MEY} B_{\infty} e^{(-b' F_{MEY})} \tag{2.44}$$

Finally, the optimum fishing effort at *MEY* (f_{MEY}) is expressed as:

$$f_{MEY} = \frac{F_{MEY}}{q} \tag{2.45}$$

Example 2.2. Bioeconomic yield-mortality model

The example to be given below (Defeo & Seijo, in press) is based on a hypothetical data set used by Caddy (1986: p. 387), which is adapted to the methodology proposed (Table 2.2). Bioeconomic information that would allow the calculations reported here on a real data set is not available, so that the results (and the estimates of mortality used) are only intended to illustrate the bioeconomic model developed and the proposed methodology of fitting the data. Input data chosen to run the model was p= $3000, q= 0.0001, and c= $ 25. The *M* value used as input for the model was found by iterating equation (2.35) and maximizing the goodness-of-fit-criteria. The highest R^2 corresponded to $M = 0.13$/yr.

Table 2.2. Hypothetical data used for fitting the bioeconomic yield-mortality model (adapted from Caddy, 1986).

Year	Yield (tonnes)	Z (1/yr)
1	7.5	0.175
2	12.5	0.170
3	19.0	0.250
4	35.0	0.440
5	40.5	0.610
6	39.5	0.795
7	30.5	1.080
8	20.0	1.170
9	26.0	0.900
10	29.5	0.790
11	27.5	0.710
12	29.0	0.470

Fig. 2.6 shows the relationship between Y and Z, fitted by the linearised exponential model. The three main *RPs: MSY*, Y_{MEY} and Y_{MBP}, are illustrated for an optimized *M* of 0.13/yr. Table 2.3 shows estimates of the mean values of the parameters, together with the 95% confidence intervals obtained by bootstrap simulations (see Chapter 7). With the artificial data set provided, the bioeconomic *RP* fell below the other two ones, in the following order: $Y_{MEY} < Y_{MBP} < MSY$. The same trend mentioned above remains valid for the remaining management parameters (Table 2.3), and thus the bioeconomic *RPs* were more conservative than the "maximum sustainable" ones, considering both the overall mean and the confidence intervals generated by bootstrap runs. It is worthy of note that Y_{MPB} as well as the corresponding mortality

rates (F_{MBP} and Z_{MBP}) were consistently below those corresponding to *MSY* and thus could be considered precautionary *RPs* (Fig. 2.6).

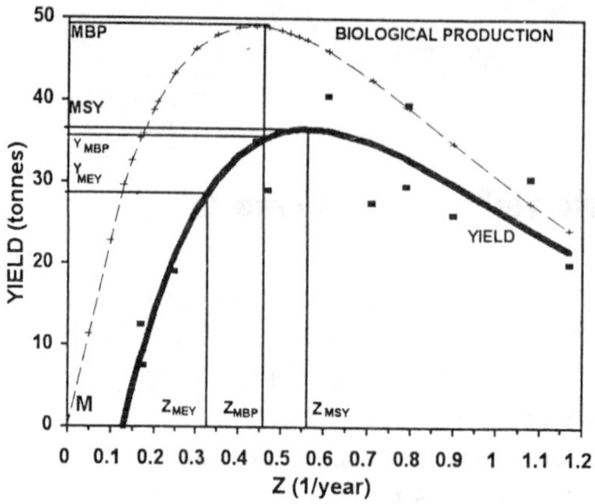

Figure 2.6. Bioeconomic *Y-Z* model: yield and biological production curves fitted to hypothetical data. The position of *MSY*, Y_{MEY}, *MBP* and Y_{MBP} is shown. A *M* value of 0.13/yr that maximized the goodness-of-fit criterion in equation (2.35) was used as input for running the model (adapted from Defeo & Seijo, in press).

Simulations involving changes in the unit cost of fishing effort (*c*) resulted, as expected, in variations in the bioeconomic *RPs* derived from the *Y-Z* model (Table 2.3). For instance, a reduction in *c* of 40% (from \$25 to \$15 per unit of effort) determined a concomitant increase in the mean bootstrap estimates of bioeconomic *RPs* of the order of 14 % for Y_{MEY}, 38 % for F_{MEY} and f_{MEY}, and 22 % for Z_{MEY}. Empirical distributions of Y_{MEY} and *MSY* obtained by bootstrapping under the two selected input values of *c* showed that Y_{MEY} fell below *MSY*, but got closer each other under a lower cost scenario. The same was valid for the remaining bioeconomic *RPs* when compared with the biological ones (Defeo & Seijo, in press). The reader is referred to Chapter 7 for a detailed discussion and application of bootstrapping to assess uncertainty.

The bioeconomic approach for fitting yield-mortality models developed by Defeo & Seijo (in press) unambiguously showed that mean and confidence intervals of bioeconomic *RPs* tended to fall in the lower bound of those corresponding to the biological model, clearly suggesting that they constitute relatively cautious *RPs* for management. The *RPs* derived from the Biological Production curve, such as the Y_{MBP} and the corresponding mortality rates (Caddy & Csirke, 1983), also constitute important benchmarks to be considered in future research on the subject, especially if it is considered that Z_{MBP} was found to be a safer target than Z_{MSY}.

Sensitivity analysis on the model to variations in unit costs resulted in changes in the bioeconomic *RPs*. As expected, they systematically increased with decreasing costs and approached the "maximum sustainable" *RPs*. This could be important in many artisanal coastal fisheries with relatively low total costs and high unit value of harvested stocks, such as shellfisheries, where the bioeconomic equilibrium is often reached at high levels of fishing effort (Seijo & Defeo, 1994b) and the corresponding F_{MEY} approaches F_{MSY}. Therefore, at very low levels of unit cost of effort, F_{MBP} could become a more precautionary *RP* than F_{MEY}. The biomass-rent trade-off can be estimated to reflect the societal cost of adopting a highly risk averse management option which departs from the rent maximizing paradigm.

Table 2.3. Mean and 95% confidence intervals (percentile approach) of the *RPs* derived from the bioeconomic *Y-Z* model, estimated by bootstrap. B_∞, *MSY*, Y_{MBP}, Y_{MEY} and *MBP* are given in tonnes, while mortality parameters are given on an annual basis (after Defeo & Seijo, in press).

Parameter	c = $ 15			c = $ 25		
	Mean	2.5 CI	97.5 CI	Mean	2.5 CI	97.5 CI
B_∞	225	160	291	228	185	296
MSY	36	31	41	36	32	41
F_{MSY}	0.440	0.348	0.531	0.435	0.363	0.511
Z_{MSY}	0.570	0.478	0.661	0.565	0.493	0.641
Y_{MEY}	32	26	38	28	22	34
F_{MEY}	0.258	0.234	0.283	0.187	0.168	0.203
Z_{MEY}	0.388	0.364	0.413	0.317	0.298	0.333
MBP	48	40	56	49	42	57
Y_{MBP}	35	31	40	35	32	40
F_{MBP}	0.375	0.283	0.466	0.352	0.281	0.429
Z_{MBP}	0.505	0.413	0.596	0.482	0.493	0.559
f_{MSY}	4,395	3,476	5,314	4,349	3,527	5,171
f_{MEY}	2,584	2,339	2,828	1,867	1,690	2,044

A simple approach to formulation of risk-averse management strategies was explored by Defeo and Seijo (in press), using decision theory (Schmid, 1989: see Chapter 7) jointly with the bioeconomic Y-Z approach developed here. For this purpose, the concepts of *Maximax*, *Maximin* and *Minimax* were recognised as powerful tools for choice under uncertainty, because they seem to be well adapted for formulation of risk-averse management strategies and precautionary fisheries management (FAO, 1995a, Pérez & Defeo, 1996). An alternative risk analysis could be carried out by using the probability density functions of Y_{MEY} and *MSY* generated by bootstrapping against the corresponding mortality rates used as control variables, in the way described by Caddy & Defeo (1996).

Yield-mortality models: a closing comment

In our view, yield-mortality models have some advantages over the classic catch-effort models because (see also Caddy & Defeo, 1996; Caddy, 1996):

(1) They can be considered as "output-output", *i.e.*, both *Y* and *Z* constitute outputs of the biologic and economic subsystems. Thus, errors due to poor calibration of fishing effort (input variable) in standard catch-effort models, as well as unperceived effects of changes in *q* with fishing intensity and biomass, might be reduced using this approach.

(2) Values calculated from the logistic model for the total mortality rate at maximum biological production Z_{MBP} tend to fall in the low percentiles of the Z_{MSY} cumulative distribution, thus constituting a relatively cautious reference point for management. Depending on the unit cost of effort, Z_{MBP} is even more cautious than Z_{MEY}.

(3) Unless there have been very considerable annual changes in fishing effort, the successive annual points in a *Y-Z* plot would not show the sharp jumps from left to right hand sides of the

yield curve, characteristic of catch-effort production models with wide departures from equilibrium.

(4) The bioeconomic model shown here assumes "pseudo-equilibrium conditions" (*sensu* Caddy, 1996: p. 219). Nevertheless, Z values derived from catch curves and multi-age group analysis more closely represent past and present impacts of fishing on all harvested year classes than do annual values of fishing effort, thus providing robustness with respect to departures from equilibrium.

A stochastic dynamic model following the systems science approach could be alternatively formulated to compare the performance of both dynamic and static approaches and to evaluate, under the light of model assumptions, which of them will prove most effective and useful for management advice. A multiple criterion optimization approach could also be developed for one or more sets of policy goals and management targets, in order to reflect the willingness of the decision maker to allow for tradeoffs among performance variables (Díaz de León & Seijo, 1992; Seijo *et al.*, 1994c: see Chapter 5).

2.4. Age-structured bioeconomic models

Age structured models consider factors affecting biomass through time, such as growth, recruitment and mortality, in a population homogeneously distributed in space and time. These models are based on the static model of Beverton & Holt (1957), and explicitly include the age structure of the population. The Beverton & Holt model and subsequent variations, assume that recruitment is independent of stock size and that it is not affected by variations in fishing intensity. Moreover, it relies on the "Dynamic Pool Assumption", which allows a unit stock to be treated as perfectly mixed age groups with homogenous distribution and equal probability of capture within the distribution area, before and after applying fishing effort. Growth and mortality parameters are the same for the entire area, and constant for the entire life span of the species (see Hancock, 1973 and Seijo *et al.*, 1994b for details).

An alternative approach to static models considers variations in population structure through time, based on the dynamic accounting of inflows and outflows of individuals to each age of the population structure. The incorporation of recruits is dynamic, allowing for a seasonal analysis of recruitment and its distribution (Seijo, 1986; Seijo & Defeo, 1994b). In the dynamic model, changes in the number of individuals through time can be defined as:

$$\frac{dN_i}{dt} = S_{i-1}(t)N_{i-1}(t) - A_i(t)N_i(t) - S_i(t)N_i(t) \qquad \textbf{(2.46)}$$

where S_i denotes the survival rate of organisms of age i and A_i corresponds to the total mortality rate (Gulland, 1983). Therefore, $S_{i-1}(t)$ can be expressed as:

$$S_{i-1}(t) = 1 - [MR_{i-1}(t) + FR_{i-1}(t)] \qquad \textbf{(2.47)}$$

where $MR(t)$ and $FR(t)$ are the finite natural and fishing mortality rates, respectively, derived from previous estimations of the corresponding instantaneous rates of natural and fishing mortality.

Rearranging:

$$\frac{dN_i}{dt} = S_{i-1}(t)N_{i-1}(t) - N_i(t) \quad \textbf{(2.48)}$$

Thus, the number of individuals in each cohort (N_i) can be obtained by integrating in the interval [*t*, *t+DT*], the number of individuals of age *i-1* that survive and grow into a cohort in time *t*, minus the total mortality rate (A_i), minus the rate at which organisms surviving cohort *i* (S_i) are incorporated into cohort *i*+1 in time *t* (Seijo & Defeo, 1994b). Using Euler numerical integration (Chenney & Kincaid, 1985), the dynamic population structure can be expressed as:

$$N_i(t+DT) = N_i(t) + \int_t^{t+DT} [(S_{i-1}(\tau)N_{i-1}(\tau) - N_i(\tau)]d\tau \quad \textbf{(2.49)}$$

$$N_i(t+DT) = N_i(t) + DT[S_{i-1}N_{i-1}(t) - N_i(t)] \quad \textbf{(2.50)}$$

In this case, the von Bertalanffy growth equation and a length-weight relationship ($W=a \cdot L^b$) are used to estimate the biomass for each age class:

$$B_i(t+DT) = N_i(t+DT)W_i \quad \textbf{(2.51)}$$

and thus total biomass *B*(*t*) is obtained as:

$$B(t) = \sum B_i(t+DT) \quad \textbf{(2.52)}$$

Fishing mortality (F_i) and yield $Y_i(t)$ by age class are obtained as in (2.26) y (2.2) respectively, but in this case both *B* and *q* are given by age class:

$$F_i(t) = \frac{Y_i(t)}{B_i(t)} = q_i f(t) \quad \textbf{(2.53)}$$

$$Y_i(t) = q_i B_i(t) f(t) \quad \textbf{(2.54)}$$

Total revenues *TR* are obtained by multiplying the unit price (p_i) by the yield estimated for each age:

$$TR(t) = \sum Y_i(t) p_i \quad \textbf{(2.55)}$$

Total costs (*TC* (*t*)) and net revenues $\pi(t)$ are obtained as in the Gordon-Schaefer model.

Example 2.3. Age-structured dynamic bioeconomic model

In the following example, the dynamic behavior of population biomass, yield, effort and revenues is analyzed for a hypothetical trawl fishery with parameters defined in Table 2.4. Simulations involve variations in the age at first capture (*tc*) and in the amount of fishing effort *f*.

Table 2.4 Parameters used for the dynamic age-structured model.

Parameter/Variable	Value
Maximum observed age	10 years
Age at first maturity	2 years
Average fecundity	5000 eggs
Age at first capture	2 years
Sex proportion	0.5
Natural mortality coefficient	0.2/mo
Curvature parameter of von Bertalanffy equation	0.5/yr
t_0 of von Bertalanffy equation	0.0
Asymptotic length $L\infty$	100 mm
Asymptotic weight $W\infty$	200 g
Selectivity parameters	L_{50}=20 mm L_{75}=30 mm
Area swept per day	0.1 Km^2
Total distribution area of the stock	10 Km^2
Maximum observed recruitment	20000000
Average price	10000 US$/tonne
Unit cost of fishing effort	75000 US$/vessel/d
Fleet dynamics parameter	0.00005

The dynamic trajectories of fishery performance variables under different *tc* values are observed in Fig. 2.7. Biomass decreases to a minimum concurrently with highest yields, 20 years after the beginning of the fishery. Decrements in biomass are more noticeable with low *tc* values, which in turn determines the lowest values of yields and economic rent. A long-term equilibrium is reached after 45 years (Fig. 2.7a to d). Maximum fishing effort is about 200 vessels for a *tc* comprised between 2 and 3 yr at *ca.* 20 years and diminishes onwards as a result of negative economic rent (Fig. 2.7c). The number of vessels at *tc* values varying from 1 to 4 yr under bioeconomic equilibrium, are, respectively, 67, 90, 115 142 (Fig. 2.7d); *i.e.,* a relatively high *tc* (*e.g.,* 4 yr) allows the fishery to support a greater number of vessels. However, an indiscriminate increase in *tc* (*e.g.*, greater than 4 years) could not justify vessels operating in the fishery. Yields and economic rent are highest with *tc* = 2 years. Certainly, the resulting dynamic biomass for high *tc* values are higher and with low variations through time. Fishing effort tends to increase proportionally to the rent generated by the fishery under different *tc* scenarios (Fig. 2.7d). In the long run, under open access conditions and with *tc* = 4, the fishery is able to support more than twice the number of vessels than with *tc* = 1 yr. The yield at bioeconomic equilibrium increases from 158 tonnes with *tc* = 1 yr to 272 tonnes with a *tc* = 4 yr (Fig. 2.7b).

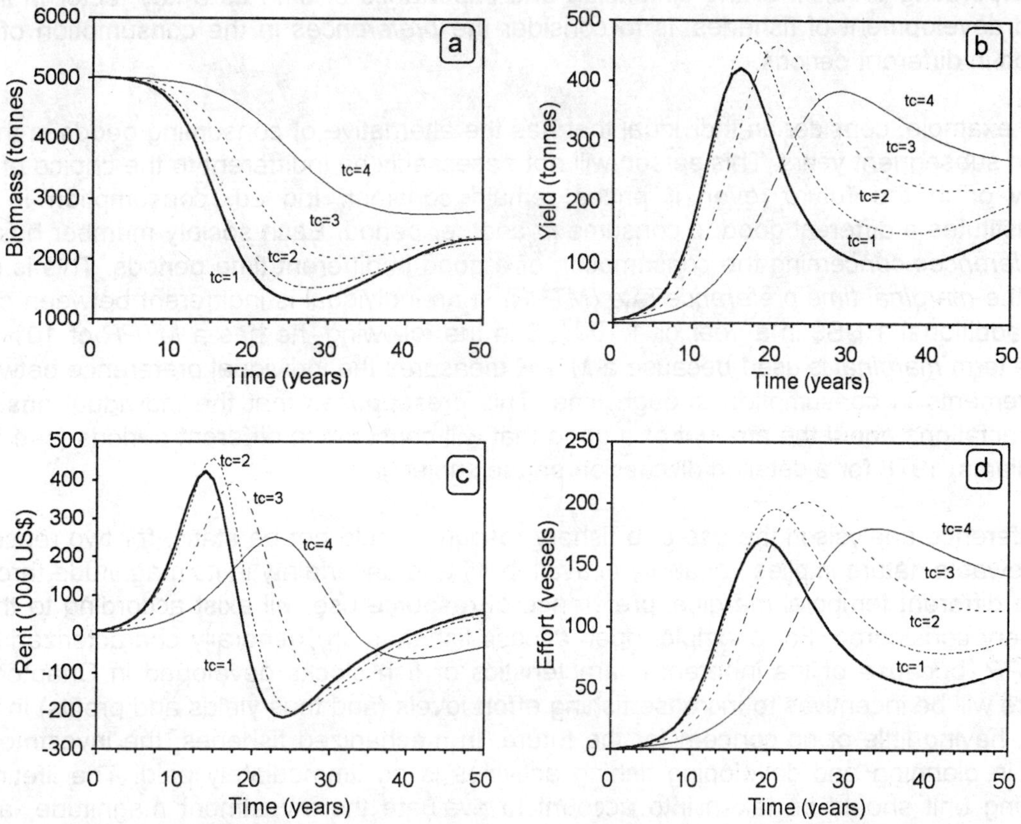

Figure 2.7. Age-structured bioeconomic model: dynamic effect of different *tc* in (a) biomass; (b) yield; (c) economic rent; and (d) fishing effort.

As can be observed from the above example, the dynamic age-structured model allows one to explore the impact of several sizes/ages at first capture. When the selectivity by size is variable, this important control variable becomes a management instrument that the global models such as the Gordon-Schaefer cannot handle.

2.5. Intertemporal fisheries analysis

Two key predictions were derived from the classical *static* bioeconomic model: 1) an open access regime leads to stock overexploitation and dissipation of the economic rent; and 2) *MEY* will occur at a lower exploitation rate than *MSY*. However, *this model ignores the time dimension in the estimation of optimal yield and effort levels*. In this section we introduce the price of time to explain the bioeconomic dynamic behavior of a fishery. We also show that the optimal exploitation rate of a fish stock could be greater or lower than *MEY* or *MSY*, depending on the intertemporal preferences of society concerning resource use.

Intertemporal preferences

Fishing effort investment decisions are related to the expectation that the fishing unit (*i.e.* vessel + gears) assures positive net revenues throughout its lifetime. An approach to the incorporating problem of the dimension and importance of time as a key factor in investment and development of fisheries, is to consider the *preferences* in the consumption of a certain good in different periods.

For example, consider an individual that has the alternative of consuming goods in the present or in subsequent years. This person will not necessarily be indifferent to the choice of spending now or in the future, even if prices remain constant. Indeed, consumption in a period constitutes a different good to consume in another period. Each society member has *temporal preferences* concerning the consumption of a good in different time periods. This is measured by the *marginal time preference rate* (*MTPR*). If an individual is indifferent between consuming an additional 1 US$ in a year or 1.10 US$ in the following, he has a *MTPR* of 10% per year. The term *marginal* is used because a *MTPR* measures the individual preference between small increments in consumption through time. This presupposes that the individual has dissimilar expectations about the amount of a good that will consume in different periods (see Sudgen & Williams, 1978 for a detailed discussion on the subject).

Preference analysis in the use of a fishery resource could not be static, for two reasons: 1) its renewable nature implies variability in availability and uncertainty in its magnitude through time; 2) a different temporal marginal preference of resource use will exist according to the type of fishery considered. For example, open access fisheries are generally characterized by a high *MTPR*, because of the inherent characteristics of fish stocks developed in Chapter 1. Thus, there will be incentives to increase fishing effort levels (and thus yields and profits) in the short-run, having little or no concern for the future. In mechanized fisheries, the investment carried out in planning and developing fishing activities is not immediately paid. The lifetime of the fishing unit should be taken into account to evaluate the investment magnitude, as well as present and future costs, and the probable revenues derived from fishing. In these cases, it is probable that, under precautionary management schemes (*e.g.* limited entry), a low *MTPR* occurs, in order to favor investments and to sustain the resource in the long run.

Neutral, positive and negative preferences

Consider a fisher A who has to decide on how to distribute his consumption activities in two time periods t_1 and t_2. (Randall, 1981). Total consumption in each period (Ψ_t) could be defined as a budget in each period, that is, Ψ_{t1} in t_1 and Ψ_{t2} in t_2. Assume that the fisher receives an income Q_1 in t_1 and Q_2 in t_2, being $Q_1 = Q_2$. Figure 2.8 shows the indifference curve I_a for fisher A, which defines his time preferences in resource use in two successive time periods. *WW* is the intertemporal budget line, where $W = Q_1 + Q_2$. *WW* has a negative slope = -1, and thus the income could be transferred for one period to another on a one to one basis. The indifference curve passes through a common point represented by Q_1 and Q_2. Fisher A has a *neutral time preference* if he prefers the same consumption in t_1 as in t_2 (with $\Psi_{t1} = \Psi_{t2}$ and $Q_1 = Q_2$).

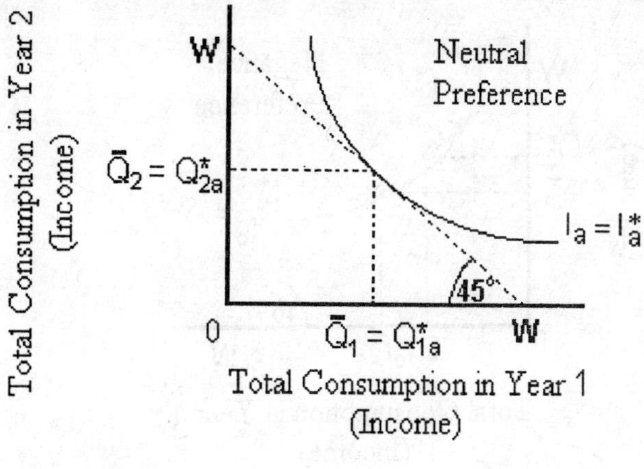

Figure 2.8. Intertemporal neutral preference (adapted from Randall, 1981).

Now consider a fisher B and his respective utility function (indifference curve I_b) in two-time periods t_1 and t_2 (Fig. 2.9). If consumption could be reallocated between periods (*e.g.* if it is possible to transfer incomes), fisher B could transfer part of his consumption from t_2 to t_1, and his total consumption would be Q^*_{1b} + Q^*_{2b}. Fisher B has a *positive time preference* or a *high MTPR*, since he prefers to consume immediately, rather than in subsequent periods, *i.e.*, he would sacrifice a relatively high amount of a good to be consumed in the future in exchange for an increment in the current consumption.

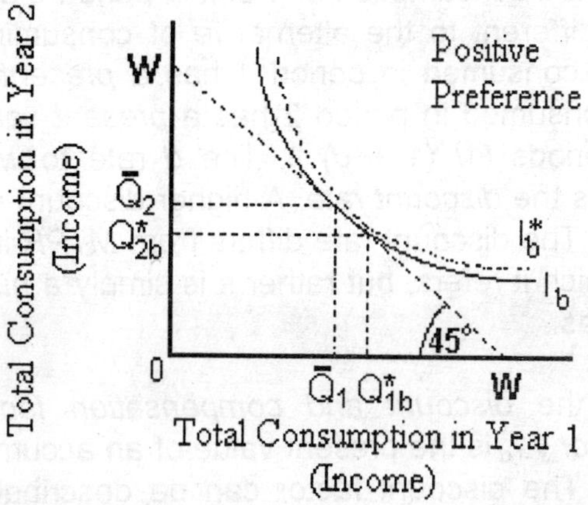

Figure 2.9. Intertemporal positive preference (adapted from Randall, 1981).

Fisher C (Fig. 2.10) has a *negative time preference* or a low *MTPR*. He will transfer part of his consumption in the current period to the subsequent one, in such a way that his consumption will be Q^*_{1c} + Q^*_{2c}. Thus, his optimal intertemporal consumption is achieved at the tangent between *WW* and the indifference curve I^*_c.

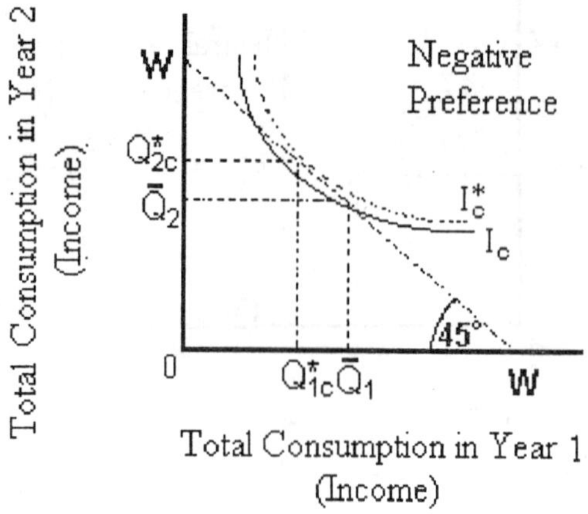

Figure 2.10. Intertemporal negative preference (adapted from Randall, 1981).

Present value and discount rate

The *present value* of a flow of future revenues allows for comparisons of money during different time periods. The *discount rate (d)* is used for this purpose. Individuals with different time preferences adjust their intertemporal consumption profile so as to be indifferent between now and later. For example, suppose that an individual has a *MTPR* of *d* per time period, *i.e.,* he is indifferent between an extra consumption of 1 unit in period 0 and 1 + *d* units in period 1. Analogously, he would be indifferent to the alternative of consuming $(1 + d)^2$ extra units in period 2. Thus, an extra unit consumed in period 1 has a *present value* of (1/1+*d*) units in period 0, and an extra unit consumed in period 2 has a *present value* of $1/(1 + d)^2$ units in period 0, and so on for *t* periods $(1/(1 + d)^t)$. The *d* rate to which future revenues are discounted at present values is the *discount rate.* A higher discount rate would lead to a lower present value, and vice versa. The discount rate differs from *MTPR* in that it does not imply an interpretation of the rate to which it refers, but rather it is simply *a number*, generally constant, used in arithmetic manipulations.

Related concepts, such as the *discount and compensation factors*, could be used for calculations. The *discount factor* $v_{t,d}$ is the present value of an accumulated unit in the period *t*, when the discount rate is *d.* The discount factor can be described as a geometric regular pattern of the form:

$$v_{t,d} = \frac{1}{(1+d)^t} \tag{2.56}$$

The *compensation factor* a_d is the present value of a flow of revenues based on the accumulation of one unit in each of the *t* periods, at a discount rate *d*:

$$a_d = \sum \frac{1}{(1+d)^t} \tag{2.57}$$

where: *t* = 1, 2,...., *n*. In terms of the discount factor:

$$a_d = \sum v_{(t,d)} \tag{2.58}$$

The compensation factor is useful when the flow of costs and benefits through time *is the same.* This is rarely the case in fisheries.

The bioeconomic dynamic model and the price of time

Although the equilibrium estimators *MSY*, *MEY* and *BE* are useful benchmarks as *RPs* in the bioeconomic analysis of fisheries, their static nature diminish their reliability as appropriate management tools. Considering it extremely unlikely that the fishery system reflects equilibrium states, the dynamic fitting of the Schaefer-Gordon model should be preferred to its static counterpart, as it takes into account the intertemporal flow of costs and benefits from different fishing effort levels and dynamic biomass fluctuations. Thus, a fishery should be managed by maximizing a dynamic exploitation pattern more than by setting a specific (static) sustainable yield level. Indeed, a fishery will be economically efficient *if it maximizes the net present value of catches*. Since these are autocorrelated in time, the bioeconomic static analysis loses significance as an appropriate fisheries management tool.

The net present value of a flow of benefits and costs through time could be expressed as:

$$PV\pi = \frac{RT(t) - CT(t)}{(1+d)^t} = \frac{\pi(t)}{(1+d)^t} \qquad \textbf{(2.59)}$$

where $PV\pi$ is the present value of the net revenues $\pi(t)$.

Clark (1985) develops a bioeconomic dynamic model based on the concept of a *sole owner* attempting to maximize his profits from a fishery. This concept does not mean a monopoly, in which prices could be fixed as a result of market control. Indeed, the dynamic Gordon-Schaefer model developed by Clark assumes that the industry is a price taker (*i.e.*, prices are constant through time). The model considers the discount rate *d* in its *continuous* form. The discount factor defined in (2.56) is expressed in its exponential form as:

$$v_{d,t} = \frac{1}{(1+d)^t} = (1+d)^{-t} = e^{-\delta t} \qquad \textbf{(2.60)}$$

In this expression, δ is the *annual continuous discount rate* (Clark, 1985). According to (2.60), δ is related with *d* in the following form:

$$\delta = \ln(1+d) \qquad \textbf{(2.61)}$$

The present value of the net revenues $\pi(t)$ in a time interval (0, T) will be:

$$PV\pi(t) = \int_0^T \pi(t) e^{-\delta t} dt \qquad \textbf{(2.62)}$$

In the long run (T = + ∞), a single fishery owner will tend to maximize the present value of $\pi(t)$. Thus, substituting $\pi(t)$ in (2.62):

$$Max \int_0^\infty [pqB(t) - c]\, f(t) e^{-\delta t} dt \qquad \textbf{(2.63)}$$

The above is subjected to the differential equation that defines the classic surplus production model:

$$\frac{dB(t)}{dt} = rB(t)[1-\frac{B(t)}{K}]-qf(t)B(t) \quad \textbf{(2.64)}$$

where $f(t) \geq 0$, $B(t) \geq 0$ and that the initial biomass B_0 is known. Solving før $f(t)$ in (2.64), substituting in (2.63) and integrating by parts, Clark (1985) showed that the optimum biomass level (B_{OPT}) for a given discount rate is given by:

$$B_{OPT} = \frac{1}{4}\left\{B_{BE} + K\left(1-\frac{\delta}{r}\right) + \sqrt{\left[B_{BE} + K\left(1-\frac{\delta}{r}\right)\right]^2 + \frac{8K \cdot B_{BE} \cdot \delta}{r}}\right\} \quad \textbf{(2.65)}$$

where B_{BE} is defined as *c/pq* (see eq. 2.12). Optimum biomass B_{OPT} decreases as δ increases, and consequently will approach the biomass at bioeconomic equilibrium (B_{BE}) for $\delta \rightarrow +\infty$ (Clark, 1985).

The optimal sustainable yield (*OSY*) and optimal effort (f_{OPT}) levels for a given price of time δ are obtained by:

$$OSY = r \cdot B_{OPT}\left(1-\frac{B_{OPT}}{K}\right) \quad \textbf{(2.66)}$$

$$f_{OPT} = \frac{OSY}{q \cdot B_{OPT}} \quad \textbf{(2.67)}$$

Sustainable exploitation of a fishery resource requires that the sum of the present value of net revenues be maximized. Setting sustainable yield levels for this purpose will depend on: (a) the biological balance between recruitment, somatic growth and mortality rates; (b) dynamic fluctuations in costs and prices in a regional and international context, probably reflected in the interest rate; and (c) socio-economic and political conditions. Expectation of changes in costs, prices and stock magnitude, should be included in the bioeconomic analysis of a fishery through a weighed analysis of the probability distribution of alternative management actions, based on a dynamic stochastic approach. In this context, the selection of a specific *discount rate* value will be critical in setting an adequate exploitation strategy, and will depend on the expected variability in the bio-socio-economic variables above mentioned.

A high rate of discounting ($\delta \rightarrow +\infty$) will threaten the viability of the resource. In this case, the dynamic *MEY* will tend to *BE*. On the contrary, when resource characteristics support a long-term exploitation strategy, there is a certain stability in prices and costs, socio-economic conditions encourage investments, and the future is not discounted. Thus, as $\delta \rightarrow 0$, the dynamic and static *MEY*'s will coincide. In general, the dynamic *MEY* will fluctuate between these two extreme situations (Anderson, 1986).

The effect of δ in fisheries: an alternative view

According to Clark (1973; 1985), high δ values increase the risk of stock overexploitation. Hannesson (1986; 1987) expresses that this view *ignores the implications derived from a high interest rate in the cost of capital*, an effect previously established by Farzin (1984) for non-renewable resources. According to Hannesson, a high *d* value will increase harvesting costs, since sudden exploitation will require short-term investments in gear, equipment, etc.

Hannesson (1986) discusses the ambiguity of δ: on the one hand, it expresses the return rate required for achieving short-term profits, in such a way that high *d* values will imply high exploitation rates and a decrease in stock availability through time. On the other hand, δ expresses the *opportunity cost of capital* to be invested in the fishing unit (*e.g.* vessel, gears); thus a high δ value will imply high operation costs and therefore optimal exploitation rates at lower levels than in the previous case, promoting an increase in stock availability.

3. Ecological and Technological Interdependencies

The theoretic and analytical bioeconomic framework for fisheries management developed in Chapter 2 assumed the exploitation of a single stock by a homogeneous fishing fleet. However, sharp changes in the abundance of targeted and nontarget species, and also in the relative species composition of exploited communities, have been detected worldwide, as a result of a growing fishing intensity (see examples in Mercer, 1982; May, 1984; Pauly & Murphy, 1982). Overfishing has been observed, with a progressive decrease of the most valuable species commonly corresponding to the highest levels of the trophic chain (Pauly, 1982; Bustamante & Castilla, 1987). This has led to recognize that, in practice, fishing affects a multispecific resource (May *et al.*, 1979), harvested incidental or intentionally by fleets with different size, fishing power and gears (Gulland & Garcia, 1984; Alverson *et al.*, 1994; Anonymous, 1995; Hall, 1996, 1998).

In the last two decades, fishery scientists have taken a more holistic approach to management (Caddy & Sharp, 1986; Ströbele & Wacker, 1991; Seijo *et al.,* 1994c). For this purpose, research has been directed to evaluating the ecological and technological interdependencies, as well as the influences of the physical environment. An *ecological interdependence* is defined as occurring when two stocks have a competitive or a predator-prey relationship (Anderson, 1975a, b; Mitchell, 1982; Seijo & Defeo, 1994a; Mesterton-Gibbons, 1996). It can also account for intraspecific interactions (*e.g.* recruits and adults: Defeo, 1998). A *technological interdependence* occurs when fleets with different fishing power (*e.g.* artisanal and mechanized fleets) and/or gear types, operate on different components of a single stock or on different target species, affecting their abundance in a dissimilar form (see *e.g.*, FAO, 1978; Clark, 1985; Huppert, 1979; May, 1984). The fleet concept is here used in a wide sense, including hand-gathering techniques in artisanal coastal fisheries.

3.1. Technological interdependencies: heterogeneous fishing effort

Technological interdependencies can arise from the activity of fishing fleets with different fishing power and even different effort costs, over a single stock. The sustainable yield of two fleets (*e.g.* artisanal and industrial) can be represented as follows:

$$\frac{dB}{dt} = rB(t)\left(1 - \frac{B(t)}{K}\right) - Y_1(t) - Y_2(t) \qquad \textbf{(3.1)}$$

where $Y_1(t)$ and $Y_2(t)$ are, respectively, the yield of the fishing fleets 1 and 2 in time t.

Static analysis

Under equilibrium conditions dB/dt=0. Then:

$$rB(1 - \frac{B}{K}) - Y_1 - Y_2 = 0 \qquad \textbf{(3.2)}$$

Thus, the sustainable yield of fleet 1 can be expressed as:

$$Y_1 = rB\left(1 - \frac{B}{K}\right) - Y_2 \tag{3.3}$$

From Chapter 2 we know that:

$$Y_1 = q_1\, f_1\, B \tag{3.4}$$

$$Y_2 = q_2\, f_2\, B \tag{3.5}$$

Solving for B in equation (3.2) and substituting Y_1 and Y_2 by expressions (3.4) and (3.5):

$$B = \left(1 - \frac{q_1\, f_1 + q_2\, f_2}{r}\right) K \tag{3.6}$$

Substituting (3.6) in (3.4) and (3.5), the yield for each fleet will be:

$$Y_1 = q_1\, f_1\left(1 - \frac{q_1\, f_1 + q_2 f_2}{r}\right) K \tag{3.7}$$

$$Y_2 = q_2 f_2\left(1 - \frac{q_1 f_1 + q_2 f_2}{r}\right) K \tag{3.8}$$

and the corresponding economic rent:

$$\pi_1 = pY_1 - c_1 f_1 \tag{3.9}$$

$$\pi_2 = pY_2 - c_2 f_2 \tag{3.10}$$

The bioeconomic equilibrium *BE* for e.g. fleet 1occurs when $\pi_1 = 0$. Substituting (3.7) in (3.9):

$$\pi_1 = Kpq_1\, f_1 - \left(\frac{Kpq_1^{\,2}\, f_1^{\,2}}{r}\right) + \left(\frac{q_2\, f_2\, q_1\, f_1\, K}{r}\right) - c_1 f_1 = 0 \tag{3.11}$$

Solving for f_1 in (3.11), f_{BE} for fleet 1 is given by:

$$f_{1_{BE}} = \frac{\left[\left(1 - \frac{c_1}{Kpq_1}\right) r - q_2\, f_2\right]}{q_1} \tag{3.12}$$

The *MEY* for fleet 1 can be obtained by taking the first derivative of net revenues:

$$c_1 = Kpq_1 - \left(\frac{Kp\, q_1^{\,2} - 2\, f_1}{r}\right) + \left(\frac{q_2\, f_2\, q_1 pK}{r}\right) \tag{3.13}$$

Thus, the unit cost of fishing effort is obtained:

$$c_1 = Kpq_1\left(1 - \frac{2q_1 f_1 + q_2 f_2}{r}\right) \tag{3.14}$$

Solving equation (3.13) for f_1, f_{MEY} for fleet 1 can be expressed as:

$$f_{1_{MEY}} = \frac{\left[\left(1 - \frac{c_1}{Kpq_1}\right) r - q_2 f_2\right]}{2q_1} \tag{3.15}$$

The same reasoning can be applied to fleet 2. From equations (3.11) and (3.14), it is easy to demonstrate that f_{MEY} is half f_{BE}.

Dynamic analysis

The dynamic behavior of the stock and fishing effort can be performed by numerically solving the model. The following example illustrates the dynamic behavior of fishery performance variables of two fleets with different fishing power.

Example 3.1. Fleets with different fishing power

Given a pelagic fishery with parameters as in Table 3.1, the dynamic behavior of population biomass, yield and fishing effort exerted by an artisanal and a mechanized fleet can be described as follows:

Table 3.1. Input parameters defined for a simulation model (Seijo *et al.*, 1996) directed to evaluate the dynamic behavior of a stock harvested by two technologically interdependent fleets.

Parameter/Variable	Value
Intrinsic growth rate *r*	0.36
Carrying capacity of the ecosystem *K*	4000000 t
q artisanal fleet	0.0002
q industrial fleet	0.00035
Species price	60 US$/tonne
Unit cost of artisanal effort	15000 US$/trip
Unit cost of industrial effort	45000 US$/trip
Artisanal fleet dynamics parameter	0.00001
Industrial fleet dynamics parameter	0.00001

Results of the simulation run for a time horizon of 50 years show an expansion of the industrial fleet until biomass reaches 2 million tonnes (Fig. 3.1a, c). Beyond this threshold, the economic rent for this fleet became negative (Fig. 3.1e), leading to the exit of vessels from the fishery and a release of biomass that can be subsequently captured by the artisanal fleet (Fig. 3.1d).

Figure 3.2 shows the dynamic behavior of biomass and fishing effort exerted by both fleets. A marked decrease of stock biomass is observed during the first 10 years of the fishery, as a result of a continuous increase in fishing effort, particularly by the artisanal fleet. Both variables show long-term cycles with a time lag of 5 years, determined by the delay in investment according to stock fluctuations (Fig. 3.2a). Amplitude of oscillations of both variables tends to decrease until reaching a long-run bioeconomic equilibrium (*TR* = *TC*) in biomass and in the number of vessels in the industrial (7) and artisanal (1250) fleets. In the long-run, the artisanal fleet tends to exclude the industrial one, as a result of lower operative costs.

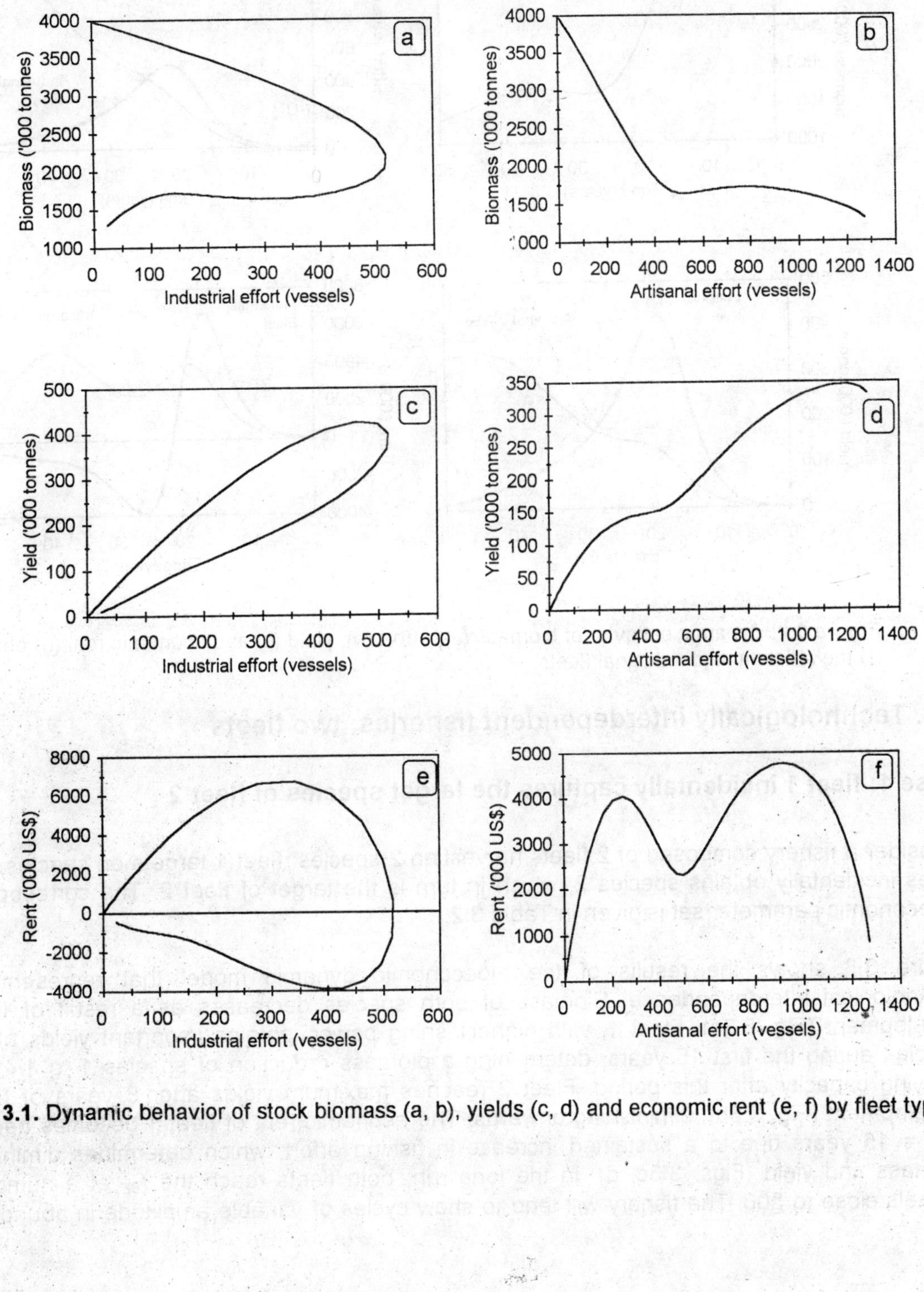

Figure 3.1. Dynamic behavior of stock biomass (a, b), yields (c, d) and economic rent (e, f) by fleet type.

This example can also be analyzed as a sequential fishery (see below), but in this case the effect of fishing fleets on population structure must be considered.

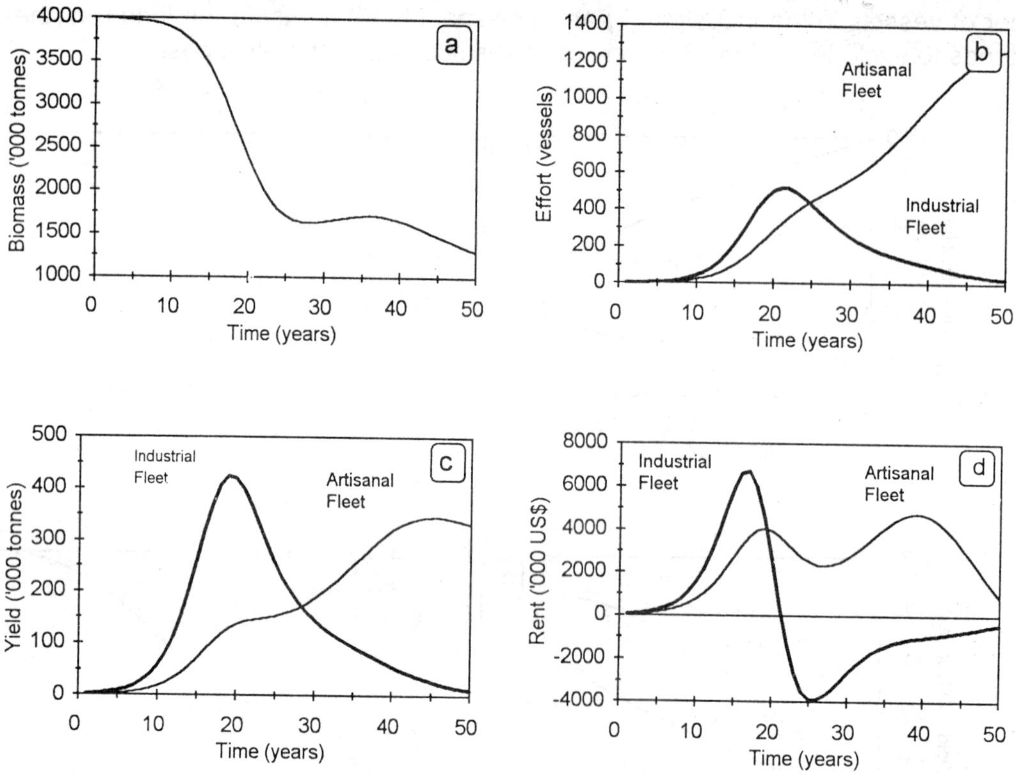

Figure 3.2. Dynamic behavior of biomass (a), effort (b), yield (c) and economic rent (d) obtained by the artisanal and industrial fleets.

3.2. Technologically interdependent fisheries: two fleets

Case 1: fleet 1 incidentally captures the target species of fleet 2

Consider a fishery composed of 2 fleets harvesting 2 species: fleet 1 targets on species 1 and takes incidentally obtains species 2, which in turn is the target of fleet 2. The corresponding bioeconomic parameter set is given in Table 3.2.

Figure 3.3 shows the results of the bioeconomic dynamic model that represents the technological interdependence. Biomass of both species decreases as a result of fishery development (Fig. 3.3a). Fleet 1, with higher fishing power, obtains important yields of both species during the first 15 years, determining a biomass reduction of species 1 to 1/4 of its carrying capacity after this period. Fleet 2 reaches maximum yields after 8 years of fishery development (Fig. 3.3b), diminishing onwards. The economic rent of fleet 1 becomes negative at t = 15 years due to a sustained increase in fishing effort, which determines diminishing biomass and yield (Figs. 3.3c, d). In the long run, both fleets reach the f_{BE} at a number of vessels close to 500. The fishery will tend to show cycles of variable amplitude in abundance, yield and revenues, according to the magnitude of fishing effort exerted by both fleets. In an ideal situation, effort level by fleet 1 should be expanded until the marginal revenues of both fleets equal the marginal cost of fishing effort in fleet 1. The same holds true for fleet 2. Effective management interventions in cyclic fisheries should be made, particularly, during the phase of increasing stock abundance in order to mitigate the effect of over-investment (see Caddy & Gulland, 1983 for useful discussions on the subject).

Table 3.2. Technologically interdependent fisheries: input parameters used in dynamic programming directed to simulate the behavior of fishery performance variables through time.

Parameter/Variable	Value
r species 1	0.36
r species 2	0.30
K species 1	4000000 tonnes
K species 2	2000000 tonnes
q species 1 fleet 1	0.0004
q species 1 fleet 2	0
q species 2 fleet 1	0.00015
q species 2 fleet 2	0.0025
Price species 1	60 US$/tonne
Price species 2	45 US$/t
Unit cost fleet 1	60000 US$/yr
Unit cost fleet 2	15000 US$/yr
Fleet dynamics parameter (1)	0.00001
Fleet dynamics parameter (2)	0.000015

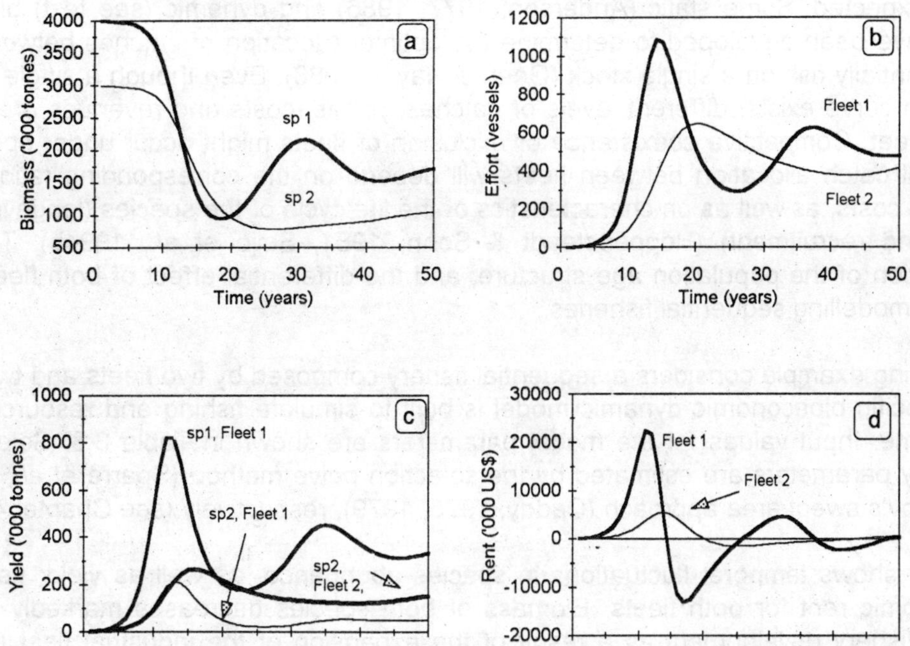

Figure 3.3. Bioeconomics of technologically interdependent fleets: (a) species biomass; (b) fishing effort; (c) yield; and (d) economic rent.

Case 2: fleets 1 and 2 affect each other

This happens when two fleets obtain incidental catches of the target species of the other fishery. Population sizes and yields of stocks *X* and *Y* are a function of the fishing effort exerted by both fleets. However, economic revenues of one fleet will depend on the effort level exerted by the other one. For fleet 1 (target species *X*):

$$\pi_1(t) = p_X Y_{X1}(f_1, f_2) + p_Y Y_{Y1}(f_1, f_2) - c_1 f_1 \quad \textbf{(3.16)}$$

whereas for fleet 2 (target species *Y*):

$$\pi_2(t) = p_Y\ Y_{Y2}(f_1,\ f_2) + p_X\ Y_{X2}(f_1,\ f_2) - c_2 f_2 \quad \textbf{(3.17)}$$

As one fleet increases its fishing effort, the equilibrium yield of the other will decrease and thus also the corresponding effort level under open access. The analysis of this case is very similar to the previous one. Because both fleets are fishing on both stocks, the operation of one will have a direct effect on the other.

3.3. Technological interdependencies: sequential fisheries

In sequential fisheries, 2 fleets spatially segregated fisheries (*e.g.* coastal artisanal and industrial at open seas) affect different components of the life cycle of one or more species (*e.g.*, shrimps: see Willmann & Garcia, 1985). Thus, competition between different resource users is expected. Some static (Anderson, 1977; 1986) and dynamic (see text) bioeconomic models have been developed to determine the optimal allocation of catches between 2 fleets that sequentially fish on a single stock (Geen & Nayar, 1988). Even though a single population equilibrium curve exists, different levels of catches, prices, costs and revenues are estimated for each fleet. Competitive coexistence or exclusion of fleets might occur under open access. An optimal catch allocation between fleets will depend on the corresponding ratios between prices and costs, as well as on characteristics of the life cycle of the species (longevity, growth, survival and recruitment) (Hoppensteadt & Sohn, 1981; Seijo *et al.*, 1994b). The explicit consideration of the population age structure, and the differential effect of both fleets on it, is critical for modelling sequential fisheries.

The following example considers a sequential fishery composed by two fleets and two species. A multispecific bioeconomic dynamic model is built to simulate fishing and resource behavior through time. Input values for the model parameters are shown in Table 3.3. Selectivity and catchability parameters are estimated by the selection ogive method (Sparre *et al.*, 1989) and the Baranov's swept area approach (Caddy, 1975, 1979), respectively (see Chapter 4).

Figure 3.4 shows temporal fluctuations in species abundance, as well as yield, fishing effort and economic rent for both fleets. Biomass of both species decreases markedly during the phase of fishery development as a result of the expansion of the industrial fleet (Fig. 3.4a). Catches of this fleet peak near year 20 (Fig. 3.4b), concurrently with a maximum number of vessels (Fig. 3.4c); from this year on, the fleet decreases gently until the end of the simulated time horizon (50 yr). In contrast, the artisanal fishery shows a steady increase in catches and in the number of vessels. As a result of lower operation costs, this fleet could exclude the industrial one in the long run. Increasing effort by the artisanal fleet could cause recruitment overfishing, with the consequent reduction of stock availability for the mechanized fleet. Concerning the latter, wide margins of revenues from years 15 to 20 determine an increase in the number of vessels, followed by an over-investment phase with subsequent economic losses (between years 20 and 25), being close to the *BE* from years 35 to 50. On the other side, the artisanal fleet presents low profits throughout the simulated period (Fig. 3.4d).

Example 3.3. Sequential fishery

Table 3.3. Input parameters of a multispecific dynamic bioeconomic model that represents a sequential fishery.

Parameter/Variable	Value
Maximum age species 1 (yr)	20
Maximum age species 2 (yr)	12
Age at first maturity species 1 (yr)	3
Age at first maturity species 2 (yr)	2
Sex ratio (both species)	0.50
Maximum observed recruitment species 1	50000000
Maximum observed recruitment species 2	100000000
Natural mortality rate species 1	0.4/yr
Natural mortality rate species 2	0.45/yr
Average fecundity species 1	1200000
Average fecundity species 2	1500000
Curvature parameter species 1	0.12/yr
Curvature parameter species 2	0.19/yr
Growth parameter t_0 species 1	-0.55 yr
Growth parameter t_0 species 2	0.50 yr
Maximum length species 1 (mm)	920
Maximum length species 2 (mm)	600
Maximum weight species 1 (g)	12500
Maximum weight species 2 (g)	2400
Minimum price species 1	1500 US$/tonne
Minimum price species 2	1000 US$/tonne
Slope of price curve species 1	50
Slope of price curve species 2	5
Unitary cost fleet 1	55000 US$/vessel /yr
Unitary cost fleet 2	5000 US$/vessel/yr
Fleet 1 dynamic parameter	0.00001
Fleet 2 dynamic parameter	0.0001
Area swept by the gear fleet 1 (km²)	2.50
Area swept by the gear fleet 2 (km²)	0.18
50% - 75% length gear retention sp.1, fleet 1	450, 650
50% - 75% length gear retention sp.1, fleet 2	300, 450
50% - 75% length gear retention sp.2, fleet 1	300, 450
50% - 75% length gear retention sp.2, fleet 2	200, 275
Distribution area, both stocks (km²)	5000

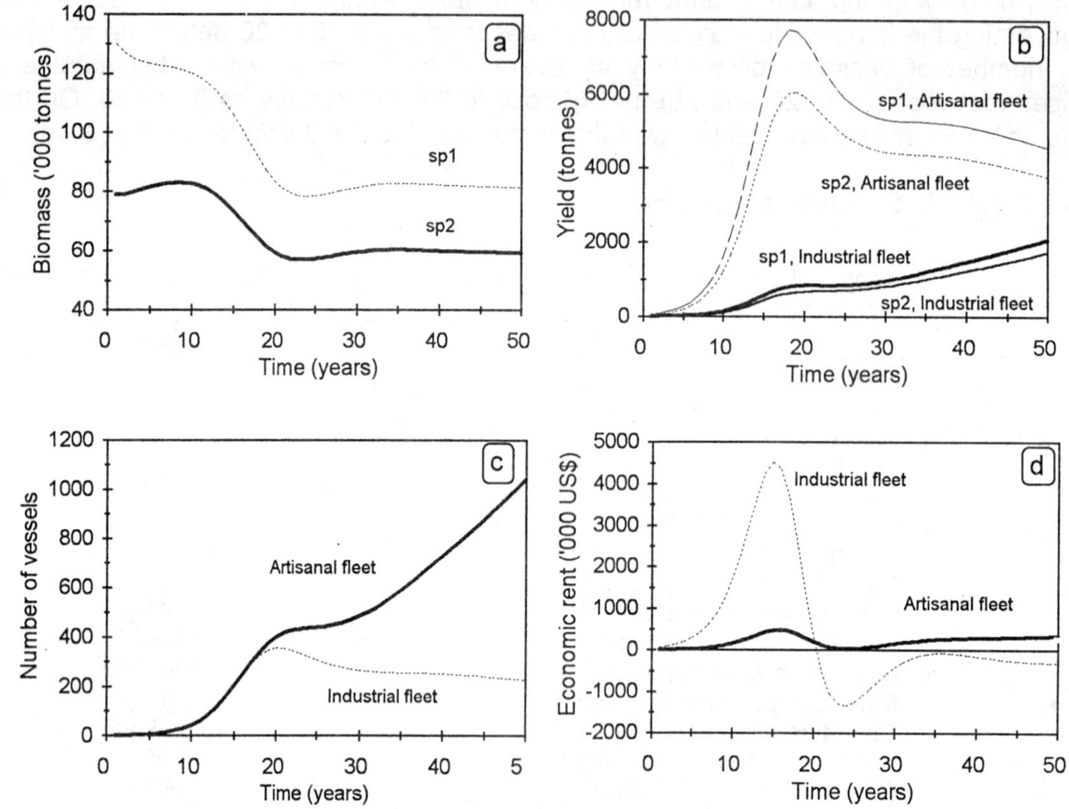

Figure 3.4. Sequential fishery. Dynamic fluctuations of: (a) biomass; (b) yield; (c) effort; and (d) economic rent generated by the industrial and artisanal vessels.

3.4. Bioeconomics of ecologically interdependent stocks

It commonly occurs that 2 independent fisheries harvest 2 stocks that interact through competition or predation. In these cases, the magnitude of effort exerted in one fishery will produce an indirect effect on the performance of the other. An optimal harvesting strategy will depend on the interaction strength between species under competition, and the dietary width of the predator in predator-prey relationships. Under open-access, the bioeconomic equilibrium in one fishery will depend on the amount of fishing effort exerted in the other.

Case 1: competition

Figure 3.5 shows the dynamic trajectories of biomass of 2 competing species, as well as the corresponding yields and economic rent generated by a single fishing fleet. In the absence of harvesting, the dominant competitor has a higher biomass than the subordinate one. As fishing effort by the dominant competitor increases (suppose that it is more valuable in the market than the subordinate), its abundance decreases, thus releasing an ecological limiting resource (*e.g.*, habitat, food). This in turn allows the biomass and yield curves to shift up for the subordinate species, until reaching an effort level above which catch also tends to decrease. The open-access bioeconomic equilibrium is reached at high effort levels that determine a low abundance of the ecologically dominant species. In this context, if the price of the subordinate species is high enough, the dominant one can be effectively driven to extinction if it is more vulnerable than the subordinate species. The economic rent is maximized at an effort level of 292 vessels.

It is worth emphasizing that the exact position of the *BE* in a fishery composed by two competing stocks depends upon the biological (*e.g.*, growth rates) and economic (*e.g.*, market prices) parameters, as well as on the interaction strength between species.

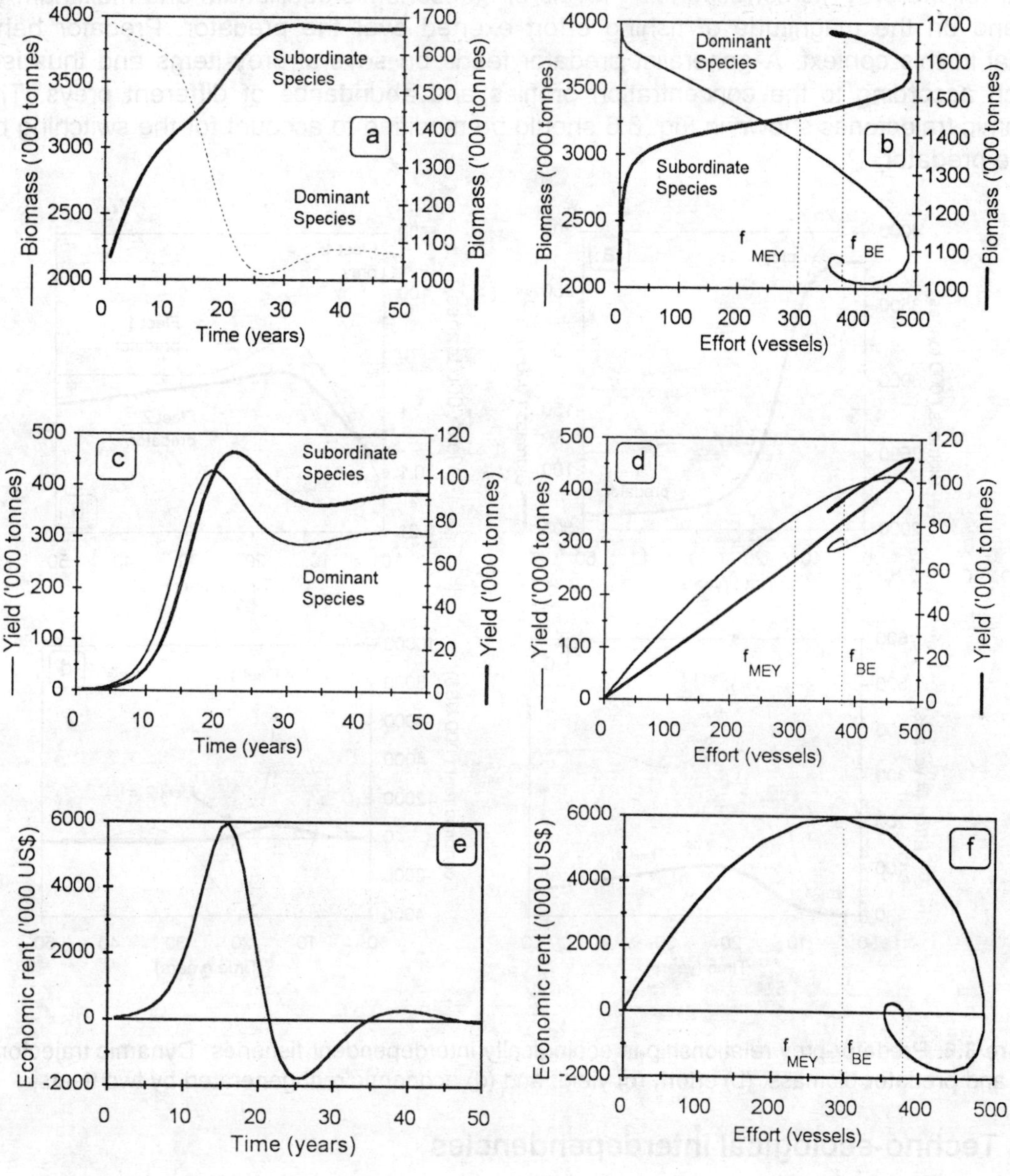

Figure 3.5. Dynamic trajectories of biomass (a, b), catch (c, d), and economic rent (e, f) generated by a fishery composed by two competing species.

Case 2: predation

In this case, an increase in fishing effort directed to the prey will decrease its abundance and thus the magnitude of resource available for the predator (assume for simplicity that the predator is specialist in its trophic behavior). Thus, increasing effort over the prey will also decrease the yield and revenues generated by predator harvesting. The reverse trend will occur for the prey: its corresponding levels of bioeconomic equilibrium and maximum yield will depend on the magnitude of fishing effort exerted over the predator. Predator behavior is critical in this context. A generalist predator feeds on several prey items and thus is able to switch according to the concentration profiles and abundance of different preys. Thus, the dynamic trajectories shown in Fig. 3.6 should be modified to account for the switching behavior of the predator.

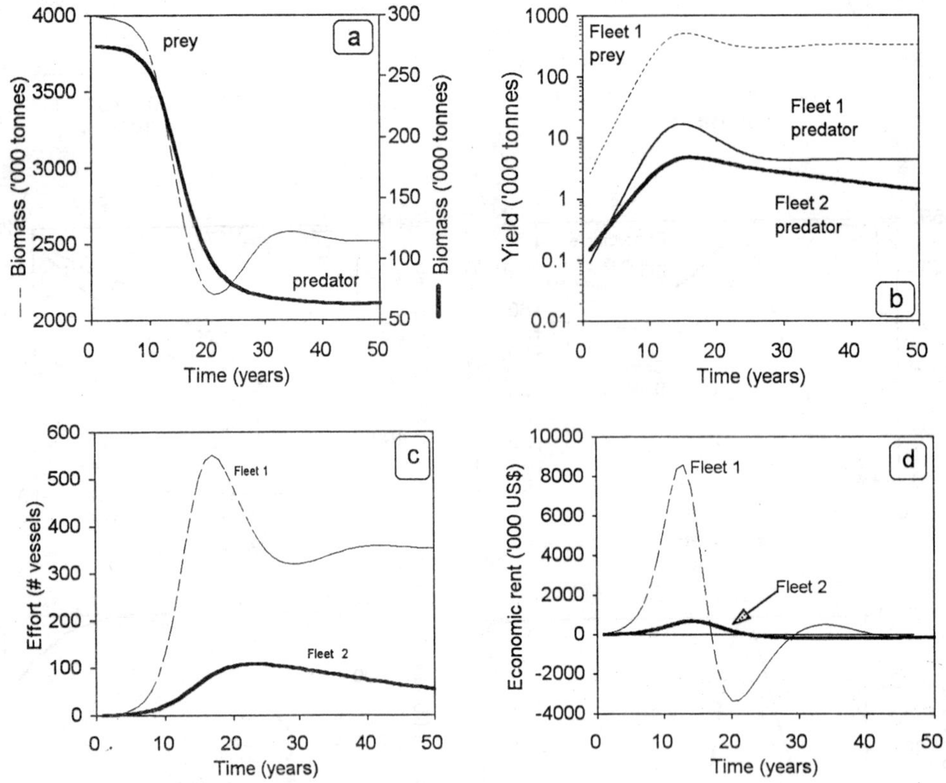

Figure 3.6. Predator-prey relationship in ecologically interdependent fisheries. Dynamic trajectories of (a) prey and predator biomass, (b) effort, (c) yield, and (d) economic rent generated by two fleets.

3.5. Techno-ecological interdependencies

A *techno-ecological interdependence* occurs when two technologically interdependent fleets harvest two interacting stocks. The multiple nature of the interaction makes difficult to analyze the dynamics of this kind of fisheries.

Case 1: competition

The Lotka-Volterra (Volterra, 1926; Lotka, 1932) and Gause & Witt (1935) models are generally used to model competition between species. In the latter, the differential equations used are:

$$\frac{dN_X}{dt} = r_X N_X - \frac{r_X N_X}{K_X} - \frac{r_X \alpha_{XY} N_X N_Y}{K_X} \tag{3.18}$$

$$\frac{dN_Y}{dt} = r_Y N_Y - \frac{r_Y N_Y}{K_Y} - \frac{r_Y \alpha_{YX} N_Y N_X}{K_Y} \tag{3.19}$$

where N_X and N_Y are the abundance of species *X* (dominant) and *Y* (subordinate) respectively; r_X and r_Y are the intrinsic rates of population growth; K_X and K_Y are the respective carrying capacities of the environment when both species growth in isolation, α_{XY} is a constant that measures the per capita competitive effect on species *X* of species *Y*, and α_{YX} is a constant that measures the effect on species *Y* of *X*. Thus, the population increment of one species is limited by intra and interspecific effects. Here again, the dynamic behavior of one fishery depends upon the level of effort in the other, and also on the interaction strength between competitors.

Case 2: predation

The predator-prey model used to model this ecological interdependence is based on the logistic equations described by Leslie & Gower (1960). Let *X* be the prey and *Y* be the predator:

$$\frac{dB_X}{dt} = r_X B_X \left(1 - \frac{B_X}{K} - \beta_1 B_Y \right) \tag{3.20}$$

$$\frac{dB_Y}{dt} = r_Y B_Y \left(1 - \frac{B_Y}{\beta_2 B_X} \right) \tag{3.21}$$

In this set of equations, prey growth is limited by the carrying capacity of the system, *K*, and also by the predation term $\beta_1 B_Y$. Growth of the predator (species *Y*) population is a function of its intrinsic growth rate and prey number. Constant β_2 relates the number of preys with the maximum biomass that the predator is able to reach, constrained by *K*.

The following example is based on a computer model (Seijo *et al.*, 1996) that simultaneously considers a technological and an ecological (predation) interdependence (Table 3.4). Dynamic fluctuations in prey and predator biomass shown here are not the classic ones found in the ecological literature (Begon *et al.*, 1990), because the fishing fleets are technologically interrelated. Both stocks decrease with the increasing fishing effort applied during the first 15 years of fishery development (Fig. 3.7a). Fishing effort exerted by fleet 1 on prey also impacts predator biomass during this initial period, declining afterwards (Fig. 3.7b). The marked increase of fleet 1 is a response to the high yields achieved both on prey (target) and predator (incidental) (Fig. 3.7c). As a result, the economic rent for fleet 1 during the former 15 years is much higher than for fleet 2, which targets exclusively on the predator and always works close to the bioeconomic equilibrium (Fig. 3.7d). Biological and economic parameters are crucial to define the dynamic trajectories of the interdependencies. In this case for example, depleting a prey can reduce the abundance of predators, but not necessarily vice versa.

Table 3.4. Techno-ecological interdependence. Parameters defined at the beginning of the simulation run directed to evaluate the dynamic behavior of a prey and a predator captured by 2 technologically interdependent fleets.

Parameter/Variable	Value
r prey	0.36
r predator	0.15
K prey	4000000 tonnes
K predator	275000 tonnes
q prey: fleet 1	0.0004
q prey: fleet 2	0.0
q predator fleet 1	0.0002
q predator fleet 2	0.0004
Unit price of prey	60 US$/tonne
Unit price of predator	275 US$/tonne
Unit cost fleet 1	60000 US$
Unit cost fleet 2	9000 US$
Fleet 1 dynamic parameter	0.00001
Fleet 2 dynamic parameter	0.000015
β_1 (predation constant)	0.00000001
β_2 (constant)	0.069

3.6. Multispecies fisheries and experimental management

Knowledge of the magnitude of the ecological and technological interdependencies facilitates the prediction of biomass fluctuations through time and therefore the net revenues derived from fishing. The response of a community to fishing pressure depends on its complexity (*sensu* Cohen, 1987), that is, the interaction strength between species and the functional role of the exploited species (Sainsbury, 1988; Lubchenco *et al.*, 1995; Botsford *et al.*, 1997). For example, changes in community structure might be different according to the trophic spectrum (specialist or generalist) and efficiency of an exploited predator, and the magnitude of interactions between preys (if they compete or not and if the competition is symmetrical or not). Moreover, harvesting a dominant competitor will tend to increase the diversity of a community, while the exploitation of a keystone species could lead to a simplification of the community and decrease in biodiversity (Paine, 1966; Durán & Castilla, 1989). According to exploitation levels, the magnitude of the interdependencies could be modified and the corresponding management schemes altered.

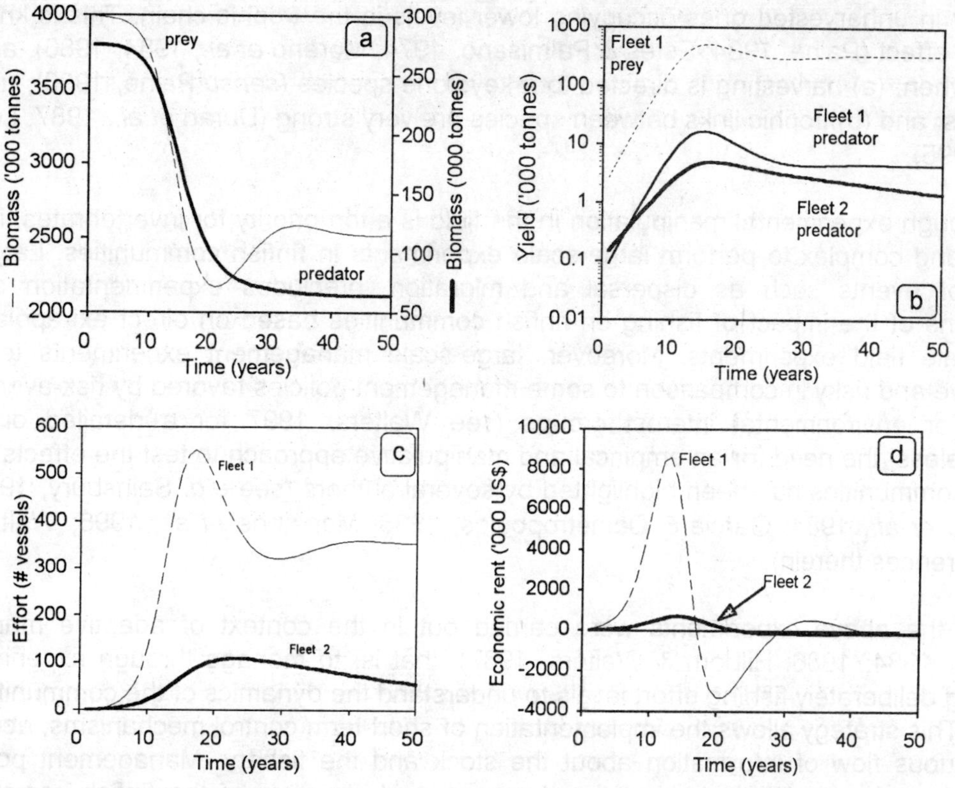

Figure 3.7. Techno-ecological interaction: stocks with a predator-prey relationship captured by 2 technologically interdependent fleets.

At least for sedentary or sessile shellfishes, improved understanding of the effects of fishing on ecological communities comes from experimental manipulation of populations and fishing effort in the field (Jamieson & Caddy, 1986; Cobb & Caddy, 1989; Defeo, 1993a, 1996; 1998; Castilla, 1994). Experimental management constitutes a useful way to determine patterns of shellfish response in relation to magnitude of fishing pressure and of linkages and strengths of ecological interactions (Defeo & de Alava, 1995). These species are particularly amenable for experimentation: the low or null mobility allows performing localized experiments with different levels of stock abundance and fishing intensity. Moreover, easy design and manipulation features of experimental plots facilitate the evaluation of population responses that might accompany dissimilar fishing levels. The low exchange of organisms among experimental replicates is an additional useful feature.

In the above context, recent experimental studies have demonstrated that the structure of harvested communities of rocky shores drastically differs from pristine ones, and that varying harvest intensity on shellfishes of different trophic levels could produce different community structures. Intertidal benthic communities protected or with minor human interference have been compared with those where man has exerted a persistent influence in the system (Castilla & Durán, 1985; Hockey & Bosman, 1986; Bosman *et al.*, 1987; Bustamante & Castilla, 1990). Results indicated that the effect of man was not only evident in targeted species, but also indirectly in unharvested ones occupying lower levels in the trophic chain. This is known as a cascade effect (Paine, 1984; Estes & Palmisano, 1974; Moreno *et al.*, 1984; 1986), and mainly occurs when: (a) harvesting is directed to a keystone species (*sensu* Paine, 1980), usually top predators; and (b) trophic links between species are very strong (Durán *et al.*, 1987; Lubchenco *et al.*, 1995).

Even though experimental manipulation in the field is a top priority for invertebrates, it is highly difficult and complex to perform large-scale experiments in finfish communities. Large spatial scales of events such as dispersal and migration, precludes experimentation and even predictions of the impact of fishing on finfish communities based on direct extrapolation from small-scale field experiments. Moreover, large-scale management experiments tend to be expensive and risky in comparison to some management policies favored by risk-averse policy-makers or environmental interest groups (see Walters, 1997 for a detailed discussion). Nevertheless, the need for an empirical and manipulative approach to test the effects of fishing on fish communities has been highlighted by several authors (see *e.g.* Sainsbury, 1987, 1988; Sugihara *et al.*, 1984; Garcia & Demetropoulos, 1986; Mapstone *et al.*, 1996; Walters, 1997 and references therein).

Most of the above experiments were carried out in the context of adaptive management (Walters, 1984; 1986; Hilborn & Walters, 1987), that is, to manage through experimentation, changing deliberateiy fishing effort levels to understand the dynamics of the community and the fishery. This strategy allows the implementation of short-term control mechanisms, according to a continuous flow of information about the stock and the fishery. Management policies are improved, and uncertainties about the dynamics and structure of the finfish community are reduced, as additional information becomes available (Sainsbury, 1987, 1988). This approach is particularly useful in cases when the overall increase in fishing activity has not been accompanied by a corresponding increase in scientific and fishery data, and the relative absence of demographic and fisheries studies may lead to inadequate fishery management advice.

The impact of fishing in the structure of an ecological community might depend also on the number of species that are marketable, and on the corresponding unit prices. For example, the net revenues derived from fishing could be maximized by deliberately overexploiting one species in order to produce the increase of a subordinate competing species with higher market value. Existing market conditions could also lead to depletion of the most commercially profitable prey species to such a low population size that the fishery for the other interdependent (predator) stock could be economically unfeasible. Recent investigations do not integrate humans as highly specialized predators but rather they consider their generalist behavior, as closed seasons/areas and other regulatory measures are being imposed to the traditionally exploited resources (Smith & McKelvey, 1986).

In summary, the fishery, the ecological interactions, the physical environment and the dynamic development of the fishing sector have differential effects on fish stocks. Thus, basic biological and experimental studies, conducted at different spatial and temporal scales, could provide the only valid alternative to predict the bioeconomic effects derived from ecological and technological interdependencies.

4. The Systems Science Approach in Fisheries Bioeconomics

As mentioned in Chapter 1, a critical step in the development of a management plan is the elaboration of a mathematical model. A useful tool for fisheries modelling is based on the systems simulation approach (Manetsch & Park, 1982; Seijo 1987, 1989; Seijo & Defeo, 1994b). In this Chapter we develop the main steps involved in the process of systems modelling. Particular emphasis is given to the application of this methodology to fisheries, detailing the main components or subsystems of a fishery, and the interactions among them.

4.1. The systems simulation approach

The system simulation approach is a problem-solving process through which particular time solutions of a mathematical model are arrived at, based on specific assumptions regarding input variables, parameters and causal relationships between them (Manetsch & Park, 1982). It comprises the following steps (Fig. 4.1):

(a) A clear definition of fishery information needs.
(b) Fishery characterization, in terms of resource and fishing effort dynamics, ecological and technological interdependencies and management instruments.
(c) Mathematical modelling of the fishery components or subsystems.
(d) Data collection, from both primary and secondary sources, needed to estimate parameters and fit equations of the mathematical model.
(e) Development of a computer model to solve numerically the mathematical model.
(f) Stability and sensitivity analyses for the computer model.
(g) Model validation.
(h) Evaluation of the bioeconomic impacts of alternative management strategies.

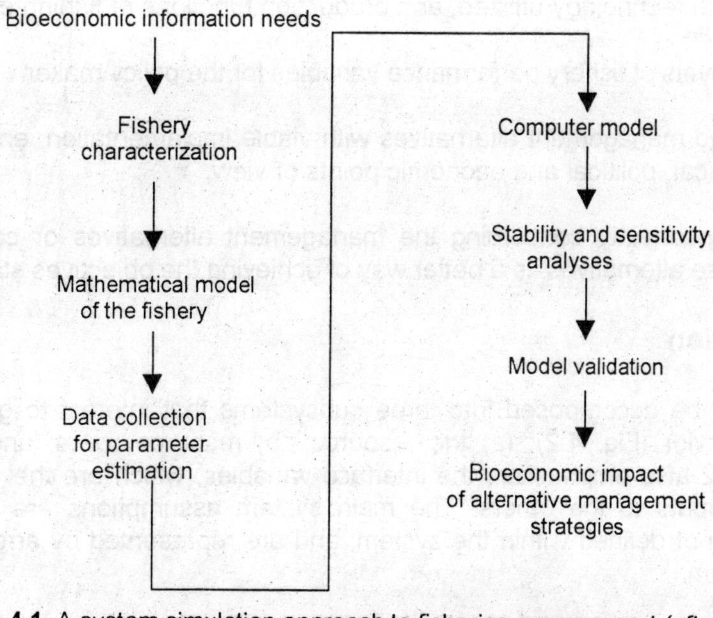

Figure 4.1. A system simulation approach to fisheries management (after Seijo, 1989).

The approach can be extended to integrate the bioeconomic model into a linear/nonlinear optimization algorithm that could involve single or multiple management criteria. This strategy allows one to generate a management vector that minimizes the difference between the performance variable levels desired by the policy maker and those generated by the model (see Chapter 5).

Identification of bioeconomic information needs

A fishery research program begins with the recognition of some management problem related to bioeconomic observations on fishery performance (*i.e.,* spatial and temporal patterns in stock abundance and intensity of fishing effort), and the search for mechanisms (management strategies) designed to achieve a sustainable fishing activity. The following approach could be useful to identify the relevant bioeconomic information required to address the management problem:

a) State clearly the management problem to be addressed, including observations about fishery performance and the person(s) involved, e.g. fishers, policy makers, or both (Ackoff, 1962; Seijo, in press).

b) Identify the management context of the fishery through the following types of parameters/ variables (Seijo, 1986):
   - *Exogenous*: environmental variables, species price.
   - *Overt controllable*: policy variables, which can be managed during system operation to alter the performance of the system in providing desired outputs.
   - *Overt necessary*: variables required in order for the system to function (*e.g.,* gas-oil, fish bait, ice and food).
   - *System design* parameters: attributes of the system structure that have an impact upon the system desired output. Includes a selected classification of fishers groups according to the technology utilized, and production functions of fishing effort.

c) Specify the desired levels of fishery performance variables for the policy maker.

d) Determine at least two management alternatives with viable implementation, enforcement and execution from physical, political and economic points of view.

e) Specifying a state uncertainty concerning the management alternatives or combinations of different levels of these alternatives, is a better way of achieving the objectives stated in (c).

Fishery characterization

The fishery system can be decomposed into three subsystems that interact to give the overall system its unique behavior (Fig. 4.2): (a) the resource; (b) resource users; and (c) resource management. Figure 4.2 also emphasizes the interface variables, which are the outputs of one subsystem acting as inputs to the others. The main system assumptions are considered as exogenous parameters not defined within the system, and are represented by arrows without an origin in the block diagram.

Resource subsystem. Includes: (1) aspects of the life cycle of the species, such as reproductive biology and recruitment, growth and mortality dynamics; (2) environmental factors affecting abundance and spatio-temporal distribution; and (3) ecological interdependencies.

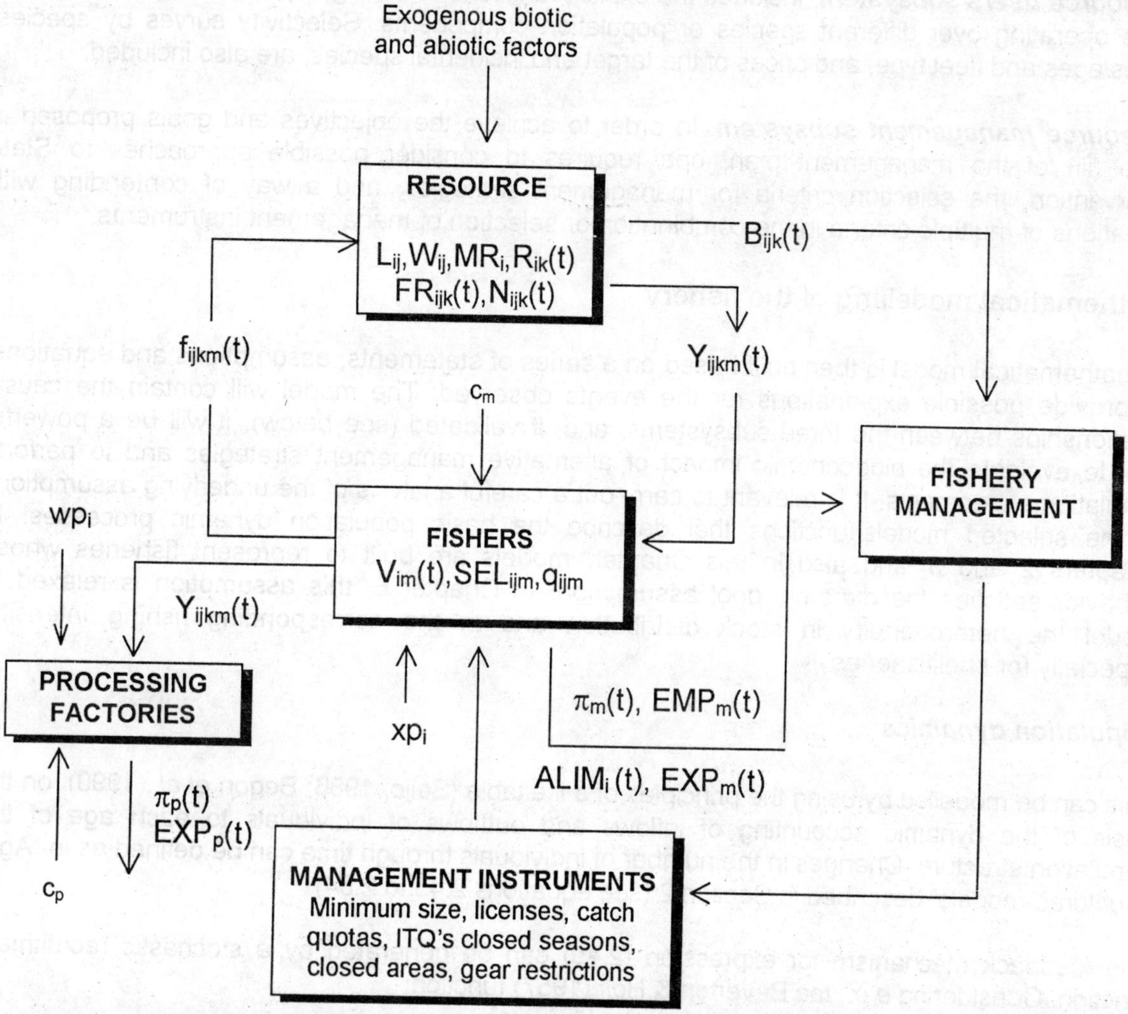

$ALIM_i(t)$ = fish for subsistence
$B_{ijk}(t)$ = biomass
c_m = unit cost of effort
c_p = processing costs
$EMP_m(t)$ = employment
$EXP_m(t)$ = export earnings, harvesting sector
$EXP_p(t)$ = export earnings, processing sector
$f_{ijkm}(t)$ = fishing intensity
$FR_{ijk}(t)$ = fishing mortality rate
MR_i = natural mortality rate

L_{ijk} = individual length
$N_{ijk}(t)$ = number of individuals
xp_i = ex-vessel price
wp_i = wholesale price
q_{ijm} = catchability coefficient
$\pi_m(t)$ = net revenues
SEL_{ijm} = gear selectivity
$V_{im}(t)$ = number of vessels
W_{ij} = individual weight
$Y_{ijkm}(t)$ = catch
$R_{ik}(t)$ = recruitment

where: i = species; j = age; k = site; m = fleet; t = time

Figure 4.2. Fishery characterization.

Resource users subsystem. Includes the explicit functions of fishing effort, decomposed by fleet type operating over different species or population components. Selectivity curves by species, sizes/ages and fleet type, and prices of the target and incidental species, are also included.

Resource management subsystem. In order to achieve the objectives and goals proposed in step (iii) of the management plan, one requires to consider possible approaches to State intervention, the selection criteria for management strategies, and a way of contending with situations of multiple criteria in the combination or selection of management instruments.

Mathematical modelling of the fishery

A mathematical model is then built based on a series of statements, assumptions and equations, to provide possible explanations for the events observed. The model will contain the causal relationships between the three subsystems, and, if validated (see below), it will be a powerful tool to evaluate the bioeconomic impact of alternative management strategies and to perform simulation experiments. It is relevant to carry out a careful analysis of the underlying assumptions of the selected models/functions that describe the basic population dynamic processes. In Chapters 2 and 3, and also in this Chapter, models are built to represent fisheries whose behavior satisfies the dynamic pool assumption. In Chapter 6, this assumption is relaxed to model the heterogeneity in stock distribution and in the corresponding fishing intensity, especially for shellfisheries.

Population dynamics

This can be modelled by using the principles of a life table (Seijo, 1986; Begon *et al.*, 1990), on the basis of the dynamic accounting of inflows and outflows of individuals to each age of the population structure. Changes in the number of individuals through time can be defined as in "Age-structured models" described in Section 2 (see equations 2.45 to 2.54).

The feedback mechanism for expression (2.49) can be generated by a stochastic recruitment function. Considering *e.g.*, the Beverton & Holt (1957) function:

$$R_i(t) = \frac{HS_i(t)\,Rmax_i}{\left(\frac{Hmax_i}{2} + HS_i(t)\right)} + RN_i(t) \qquad \textbf{(4.1)}$$

where $Hmax_i$ represents the maximum number of eggs produced by the spawning stock of species *i*. $Rmax_i$ is the maximum observed recruitment, and $HS_i(t)$ is the estimated number of eggs produced by the spawning stock *i* in time *t*. $RN_i(t)$ is a normally distributed random variable with 0 mean and known variance that represents the unexplained variability by equation (4.1). Another recruitment function (see Ricker, 1975) could be used according to the analyzed species (see Hilborn & Walters, 1992; De Anda *et al.*, 1994).

$HS_i(t)$ can be estimated for each spawning period as the product of the spawning stock abundance in time *t* by the proportion of females (H_i) and the corresponding age-specific average fecundity (FEC_{ij}):

$$HS_i(t) = \sum_{j=s_i}^{MAGE_i} H_i N_{ij}(t)\overline{FEC_{ij}} \quad (4.2)$$

where $MAGE_i$ is the maximum observed age and s_i is the age at first maturity of species *i*.

Biomass for each species is calculated as follows:

$$B_i(t) = \sum_j N_{ij}(t)\overline{W_{ij}} \quad (4.3)$$

where the average individual weight of species at age $W_{ij} = aL_{ij}^b$ (*a* and *b* are parameters). L_{ij} can be estimated by the von Bertalanffy (1938) growth function:

$$L_{ij} = L_{\infty i}(1 - e^{(-kp_i(j - t_{0i}))}) \quad (4.4)$$

where L_{ij} is the length at age, $L_{\infty i}$ is the asymptotic length, kp_i is the curvature parameter and t_{0i} the theoretical age at length = 0.

As detailed described in Chapter 2, spawning and hatching periods can be modelled using the "distributed delay model", based on the Gamma probability density functions:

$$\frac{d\gamma_1}{dt} = \frac{g}{DEL_{HS}}[HS_i(t) - \gamma_1(t)] \quad (4.5)$$

$$\frac{d\gamma_2}{dt} = \frac{g}{DEL_{HS}}[\gamma_1(t) - \gamma_2(t)] \quad (4.6)$$

. . . .

. . . .

$$\frac{d\gamma_g}{dt} = \frac{g}{DEL_{HS}}[\gamma_{g-1}(t) - \gamma_g(t)] \quad (4.7)$$

where $HS_i(t)$ are the inputs to the delay process (number of eggs spawned in time *t*); $\gamma_k(t)$ are the outputs of the delay (number of eggs hatched in time *t*); $\gamma_1(t)$, $\gamma_2(t)$,..., $\gamma_{g-1}(t)$ are the intermediate rates; DEL_{HS} is the expected period of egg maturation and *g* is the order of the delay. The parameter *g* specifies a member of the Erlang family of density functions, which describes the transit times of individual entries as they pass through the delay process.

Fleet dynamics

In the long-run, variations in fishing effort through time can be modelled by applying Smith (1969) equation:

$$\frac{df_m}{dt} = \left[\sum_{ij}(p_{ij}q_{ijm}B_{ij}(t)) - c_m\right]f_m(t) \quad (4.8)$$

Short-run (seasonal) dynamics of the fleet can be modelled by the distributed delay model, in order to represent entry of vessels throughout the fishing season. Catch by species and sizes for each fleet type *m* in time *t* $Y_{ijm}(t)$ can be described as:

$$Y_{ijm} = q_{ijm} f_m(t) B_{ij}(t) + RV_m(t) \quad \textbf{(4.9)}$$

where $RV_m(t)$ is a exponentially autocorrelated random variable which accounts for the uncertainty in the catch over time, and could be generated with other appropriate probability density functions.

A catchability coefficient by species, sizes and fleet type (q_{ijm}) is estimated by using Baranov (1918) concepts:

$$q_{ijm} = -\left[\ln\left(1 - (\frac{area_m RET_{ijm}}{AREA})\right)\right] \quad \textbf{(4.10)}$$

where *AREA* is the area occupied by the stock, RET_{ijm} is the gear retention of species *i* by age *j* of the gear of vessel type *m*, defined by a gear selection ogive, and $area_m$ is the area swept per day.

The specific gear retention by size is estimated by (Sparre *et al.*, 1989):

$$RET_{ijm} = \frac{1}{1 + e^{(S1_{im} - S2_{im} \cdot L_{ij})}} \quad \textbf{(4.11)}$$

where $S1_{im}$ and $S2_{im}$ are estimated by:

$$S1_{im} = L_{im50\%} \ln\left(\frac{3}{L_{im75\%} - L_{im50\%}}\right) \quad \textbf{(4.12)}$$

$$S2_{im} = \frac{S1_{im}}{L_{im50\%}} \quad \textbf{(4.13)}$$

where $L_{im50\%}$ and $L_{im75\%}$ are, respectively, the length at 50 % and 75 % gear retention by fleet type *m*. This catchability function is not always valid (*e.g. q* is inversely correlated with stock abundance for some pelagic stocks, MacCall, 1976), and thus it is recommended to use an age/fleet specific function according to the analyzed fishery.

The cumulative economic rent received by vessel type ($\pi_m(t)$) is estimated by:

$$\pi_m(t + DT) = \pi_m(t) + \int_t^{t+DT} (TR_m(\tau) - TC_m(\tau))d\tau \quad \textbf{(4.14)}$$

where $TR_m(t)$ y $TC_m(t)$ are, respectively, total revenues and total costs by vessel type. The former are estimated by considering prices and catches of the target and incidenta' species, whereas $TC_m(t)$ considers fixed and variable costs, as well as opportunity costs of labor and capital.

Direct employment generated by the fishery (*EMP(t+DT)* are expressed by:

$$EMP(t + DT) = \sum_m (f_m(t + DT) FISH_m) \quad \textbf{(4.15)}$$

where $FISH_m$ represents the average number of fishers per vessel type *m*.

The contribution of the fishery to seafood availability in rural coastal communities through time ($ALIM_i(t+DT)$) is estimated by:

$$ALIM_i(t+DT) = ALIM_i(t) + \int_t^{t+DT} ((1-\varepsilon)\sum_j \sum_m Y_{ijm}(\tau))d\tau \tag{4.16}$$

where ε is the proportion of the catch of species *i* and fleets *m* that will go to the export market, and thus $1\text{-}\varepsilon$ is the proportion that will be destined to the domestic market. Export earnings generated by the fishery throughout the year are estimated by:

$$\mathrm{EXP}_i(t+DT) = \mathrm{EXP}_i(t) + \int_t^{t+DT} (\sum_j \sum_m p_{ij} Y_{ijm}(\tau))d\tau \tag{4.17}$$

where p_{ij} is the export price of the species *i* discriminated by age/size *j*.

A more complete model should also include the processing sector (see Willmann & Garcia, 1985).

Data collection from primary and secondary sources

The information needed to estimate bioeconomic parameters and fit equations of the mathematical model can be summarized as follows (see also Seijo *et al.*, 1991a, b, 1994a):

Information of biological parameters

. Number of individuals by age/size.
. Sex composition.
. Natural and fishing mortalities by age/size.
. Age/size specific estimates of the catchability coefficient q by gear or fleet type.
. Individual growth function and sex specific length-weight relationship.
. Age at first maturity, average fecundity, if possible, discriminated by age/size.

Information of fishing effort

. Type of vessels and engine. Gear used by fishing fleet.
. Average number of fishers per fleet type.
. Number of vessels per port and fishing season.
. Main fishing areas and estimated mean distance from port.
. Average number of effective fishing days per trip, vessel type and fishery.
. Average duration of a fishing trip.
. Type(s) of bait utilized.

Catch information

. Number of ports in which the target species is landed.
. Total annual catch by species, fleet type, fishing season and trip.

. Size composition of the catches.
. When 2 or more countries share the stock, or if foreign vessels are authorized to fish, information about catch and fishing effort must be given by fleet.

Economic information: costs and revenues per vessel type

. **Returns** by fishing trip.
- Average price paid to fishers for target and incidental species.
- Catch estimates of the target and incidental species throughout the year.

If the catch constitutes a significant proportion of the global supply of the target species, a price function (demand equation) must be estimated.

. **Costs** of fishing effort: operation costs per trip, either on a nominal (*e.g.*, fishing days) or effective (effective fishing hours) basis.

Variable costs
Oil and gas, ice, bait, food.
Vessel repair and maintenance, replacement of damaged gears.

Fixed costs
Depreciation of the vessel, engines and gear.
Interest payment from borrowed capital. Administration and insurance costs.

Opportunity costs of capital and labor. The former is defined by the net benefits that could have been achieved in the next best economic alternative of investment. Investment costs (boat, engine and gear) are required to estimate opportunity costs of capital, interest payment from borrowed capital and depreciation. Moreover, it is necessary to specify the average interest rate on loans and for equipment and harvesting expenses for the fishing sector and the bank interest rate on fixed deposits. The opportunity cost of labor is the income that could have been achieved in the next best economic activity available to fishers. Type of crew remuneration must be indicated to estimate opportunity costs, *e.g.*: (i) as a percentage of the catch per trip (shared system); (ii) as a daily salary; or (iii) as a daily salary rate in the next best option of employment available for the fishers.

Additional relevant information

Percentage of the annual catch that goes to: (a) the fishing community for subsistence purposes; (b) the local market; (c) further product processing; and (d) the foreign market.
Exportation prices of the target and incidental species.

Computer model

The computer model can be developed in any structured programming language, as QuickBASIC, Visual BASIC or C. The general structure of the program includes the following steps:

Initialization phase

a. Values are assigned to model parameters and constants.

b. State and rate variables are initialized.
c. Time is initialized: T=0.

Specification of the simulation run

d. Length of the simulation experiment.
e. Time increment (DT).
f. Time for printing output.

Execution phase

g. Time is updated: $T=T+DT$
h. State variables are computed.
i. Random variables are generated.
j. Rate variables are computed for time T.
k. State and rate variables are printed.
l. Return to (g) if the simulation experiment is not completed.

Stability and sensitivity analyses

Stability analysis consists in determining an appropriate value for the time increment DT, in order to carry out stable simulation runs of differential equations (*e.g.*, distributed delay model). If the Euler numerical integration method is used, the necessary condition for stability requires DT to be in the interval:

$$2\,\mathrm{MIN}[D_n] > DT > 0 \tag{4.18}$$

where $D_n = DEL/g$ and $MIN\ [D_n]$ is the smallest delay constant (Manetsch & Park, 1982).

As the simulation model contains feedback processes in the population structure, it is required that:

$$\frac{1}{c} > DT > 0 \tag{4.19}$$

where $c = 1/D_n$. Therefore, DT must be within the interval [1>DT>0]. In order to reduce the numerical integration error below 5 %, DT might be 0.01.

Sensitivity analysis allows observing variations in model performance under marginal changes (20% increments/decrements) in model parameters (*e.g.*, natural mortality) and initial conditions of rate and state variables (*e.g.*, initial biomass, fishing effort levels).

Model validation

A simulation model is validated if it provides a correct representation of the real system. Validation procedures vary from qualitative to quantitative tests, depending on the amount of data available and system understanding (Seijo, 1986; Rykiel, 1996). Concerning the latter, parametric and non-parametric statistical tests (*e.g.*, Kolmogorov-Smirnov test) could be used to test the null hypothesis of equality of distributions of actual and simulated variables, such as catch, effort and stock biomass (see Defeo *et al.*, 1991). Discussion of model structure and results with resource specialists, system scientists and resource managers should also be undertaken (see also Payne, 1982; Graybeal & Pooch, 1980).

A multistage validation procedure should be applied to critical stages in the model building process, *i.e.*, design, implementation and operation of the model (see Rykiel, 1996 for details). The model can be considered validated if it accurately predicts the actual data set (replicative validation) or some new or unexamined set of observations (predictive validation) (Power, 1993). Even though validation is often an essential testing process to evaluate model performance, for those models directed to "describe or systematize knowledge or to develop theory, validation is unnecessary and irrelevant" (Rykiel, 1996).

Bioeconomic impact of alternative management strategies

Once the bioeconomic model is built, it is necessary to conduct simulation experiments directed to evaluate the bioeconomic impact of different management strategies. This includes for example: (i) 20% increment in fishing effort of artisanal/mechanized fleets; (ii) extension (reduction) of a closed season; (iii) implementation of a minimum legal size; or combination of the above and other strategies.

A bioeconomic approach to fisheries management with multiple criteria, introducing a nonlinear optimization algorithm, could be integrated to reconcile economical and ecological criteria, in many cases conflicting with each other (see Chapter 6).

4.2. A numerical example

Suppose a sequential shrimp fishery is composed by an artisanal fleet that captures juveniles and young adults, and a mechanized fleet that essentially captures the adult component of the stock. A bioeconomic analyst has been requested to evaluate fishery performance under the following management instruments: minimum size at first capture, length of the fishing season and specification of the preferred months for a closed season. A limitation in the number of vessels is assumed. It is also assumed that the mechanized fleet is not versatile and therefore will pay for the fixed costs during the closed season. Since recruitment periods above the average (20% of the observed years) could occur, the manager is considering the possibility of increasing by 25% the number of licenses for both fleets. Main fishery parameters are shown in Table 4.1.

Short and long run dynamics. In the short-run, the model represents dynamically the seasonal distribution of recruitment (Fig. 4.3a) and fishing effort (Fig. 4.3b). With a fishing season of 10 months, beginning in the third month, the effect on the spawning stock is reflected in the relative magnitude of both recruitment periods: in the former, the maximum number of individuals is 13.2 millions, whereas in the second it is 7.8 millions. If the start of the fishing season is changed, the success of both recruitment periods could be affected. Analogously, the recruitment magnitude for both periods would be affected if the length of the fishing season varied. The above results allow us to combine and evaluate the effects of different starting dates and durations of the fishing season, given a known distribution of recruitment peaks, in order to maintain and, if possible, to increase the economic rent that the fishery could generate through time.

Table 4.1. Bioeconomic parameters of a hypothetical shrimp fishery.

Parameter/variable	Value
Maximum age of the species	24 mo
Age at first maturity	6 mo
Age at first capture for fleet 1 (mechanized)	3 mo
Age at first capture for fleet 2 (artisanal)	2 mo
Average fecundity	1072000 eggs
Growth curvature parameter	0.27/mo
Growth parameter t_0	-0.03/mo
Asymptotic length	245 mm
Asymptotic weight	140 g
Area swept per day fleet 1	1.41 Km^2
Area swept per day fleet 2	0.25 Km^2
Length at 50% gear retention, fleet 1	170 mm
Length at 50% gear retention, fleet 2	150 mm
Length at 75% " " fleet 1	175 mm
Length at 75% " " fleet 2	170 mm
Stock distribution area	6405 Km^2
Fleet types	2
Fleet 1 dynamic parameter	0.000001
Fleet 2 dynamic parameter	0.0000015
Maximum observed recruitment	76900000 ind
Length of the fishing season	10 mo
Start of the fishing season	Mo 3
Month of first recruitment	Mo 4
Month of second recruitment	Mo 11
Length of simulation run	3 yr
Order of the distributed delay	2 mo
Fishing days/mo fleet 1	20
Fishing days/mo fleet 2	12
Time delay of boats entry	0 d
Average time delay of recruits transit	2 mo
Unit cost of fishing effort, fleet 1	65000 ($/vessel/yr)
Unit cost of fishing effort, fleet 2	3000 ($/vessel/yr)
Minimum price (90-100/lb)	1500 ($/tonne)
Slope of the curve of prices/length	700 ($)
Incidental weighted income	318 ($/tonne)

Fishery yield decreases through time for both fleets (Figs. 4.3c, d). However, the relatively low unit cost of artisanal fishing effort allows it to generate economic rent. Figures 4.3e and 4.3f show dynamic fluctuations of costs and benefits as perceived by each fleet. The accumulated rent throughout the fishing season will determine, under open-access, potential **long-term** changes in the number of vessels. For both fleets, the number of vessels begins to decrease from the second year of the simulation run as a result of negative profits. This shrimp fishery reflects a clear trend towards overexploitation and overinvestment.

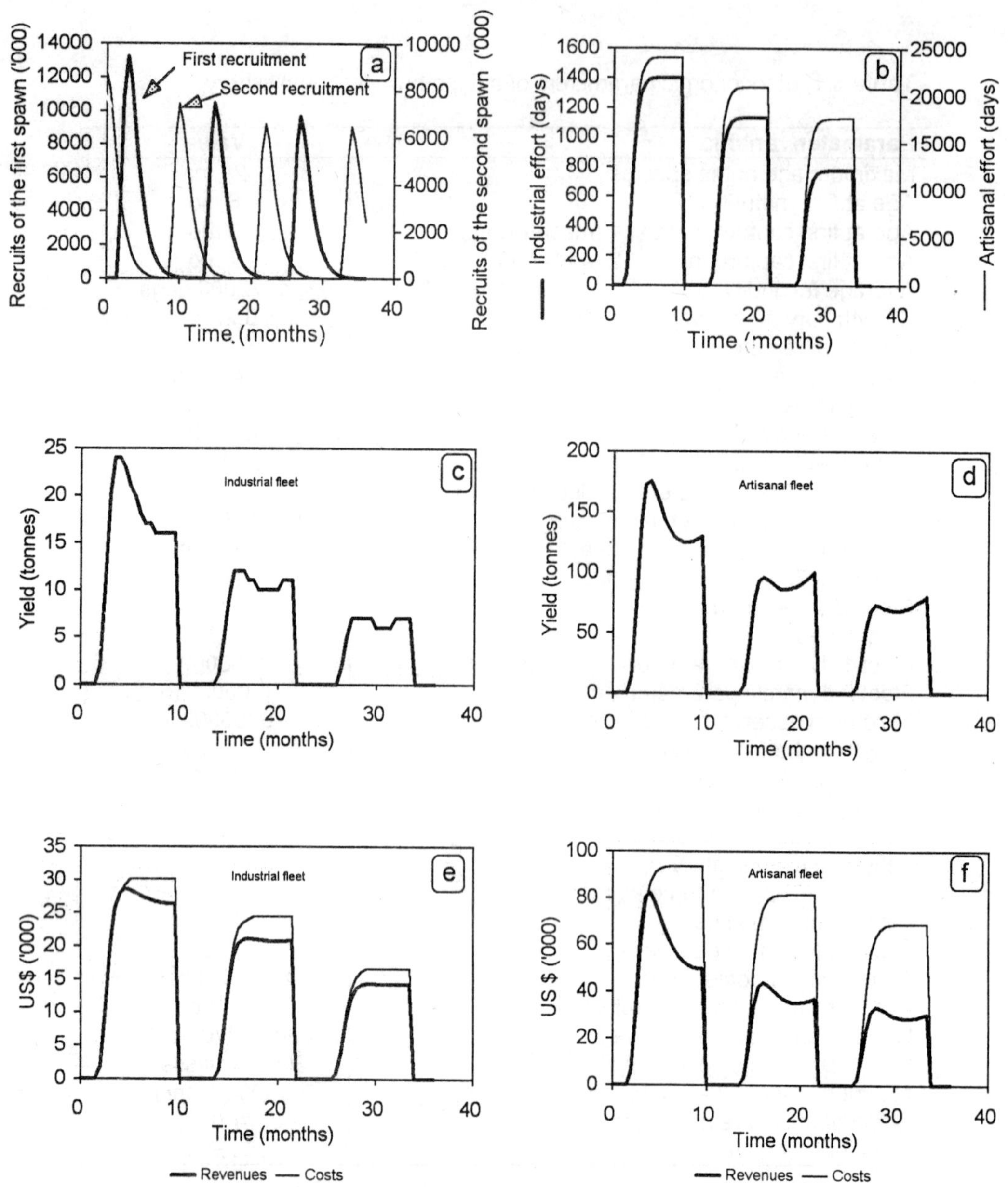

Figure 4.3. Short and long-term dynamics of: (a) recruitment; (b) fishing effort; (c,d) yields; and (e,f) benefits/costs for the artisanal and mechanized fleet of a hypothetical shrimp fishery.

5. Management

There has been an increasing trend towards the incorporation of non-monetary criteria in the bioeconomic analysis of fisheries, such as conservation of marine biodiversity, protection of endangered species and other unpriced values (existence value and option demand value). This approach needs to reconcile economic and ecological criteria, which in many cases conflict (Charles, 1989; Charles & Herrera, 1994). On the one hand, a maximization of the net present value perceived by fishers is desired; on the other hand, abundance and yield of the harvested species should be sustainable over time. In this Chapter, some fisheries regulation criteria are described, notably forms of State intervention. A bioeconomic approach introducing a non-linear optimization algorithm for fisheries management with multiple criteria, is also presented.

5.1. State intervention criteria

The following fisheries management criteria have been identified (see also Panayotou, 1983; Beddington & Rettig, 1984; Lawson, 1984):

Conservation approach

This is usually based on fishing effort regulation, under the assumption that once fishing effort is regulated, changes in species abundance could be reversible in a reasonable time period. However, the lack of long-term time series means that the results of the evaluation techniques commonly used (*e.g.* Virtual Population Analysis: VPA) don't show enough evidence to justify the reduction of effort until overexploitation occurs. Thus, there has been a risky trend towards the exploitation of stocks at levels close to overexploitation, which in many cases determined an important reduction of fishing effort levels or even the closure of the fishery, with social and economic implications.

Economic approach

In open access fisheries, the bioeconomic equilibrium is reached with increasing economic inefficiency (Clark, 1985). When a fishery is developing, a trend of declining costs occurs due to an increasing fishing power and efficiency, together with increasing knowledge of the most important fish concentrations. However, these factors tend to (a) reduce stock abundance, (b) increase harvesting costs and (c) diminish net revenues per unit of effort. When this happens, fishing areas closest to port are gradually overexploited or even depleted (*e.g.,* sedentary stocks) and the areas previously less attractive will tend to be progressively used. Thus, the bioeconomic equilibrium will be reached at high levels of stock overexploitation, at which point the lack of profits discourages entry of new vessels.

Policy makers rarely refer to the concept of economic efficiency; on the contrary, they respond more to high unemployment rates, fishery collapse and decline in income levels, with the consequent socio-economic repercussions (Maiolo & Orbach, 1982). Indeed, some stocks are exploited even at very low biomass levels, because increasing costs are compensated by an increase in the species price, as a result of a reduction in market supply. This constitutes an important drawback to the wholesale application of economic criteria.

A simple bioeconomic approach that does not consider variations in environmental factors will not provide a real representation of the fishery, especially for species highly sensitive to environmental variability as small pelagics (*e.g.* anchovy and sardine). Exogenous environmental factors affect the stock and thus the economic rent derived from the fishery. This is the reason why some fishery scientists state that the true deterministic bioeconomic equilibrium does not hold (Beddington & Rettig, 1984). Again, this precludes the application of economic criteria for fishery management.

Equity approach in resource use

Under open access conditions and decreasing stock abundance, some fishers will be more affected than others. Generally, those vessels with high autonomy and economic rent will increase harvest rates by exerting their fishing effort on distant fishing grounds. This could produce conflicts among fishers, and thus the major task in the selection of management alternatives resides in *how to favor a user' group without damaging others. Economic damage* is defined as the reduction in incomes or satisfaction of an individual as a result of a public decision (in this case a given management strategy). In this context, equity is an important social consideration by which to assess State intervention strategies; however it is difficult to implement, as equal opportunities do not guarantee an equal distribution of non-renewable resources.

The main postulate of economic welfare theory as applied to fisheries (Hannesson, 1978), establishes that the maximization of social welfare is the final purpose of fishery policy. The main underlying concept is *Pareto optimality.* A fishery management strategy is *Pareto optimal* if changes generated by management instruments allow improving the welfare of one or more fishers without worsening others. The necessary and sufficient conditions for a management strategy to be Pareto optimal are as follows:

(i) The technical substitution rate between any pair of inputs of fishing effort would be equal for all vessels and equal to the price ratio of the inputs.

(ii) It would not be possible to increase catches and economic rent generated by a species (or group of species) without diminishing catches and economic rent that other fishers would obtain by harvesting this (these) species or others that are ecological and/or technologically interdependent.

(iii) It would not be possible to redistribute catches between consumers of sea products in such a way that the welfare of a consumer could improve without diminishing the welfare of others.

By combining conditions (ii) and (iii), it is possible to derive the general condition that relates production and consumption of exploited fishing resources:

(iv) *The substitution rate for any pair of marine goods will be equal for any pair of consumers, and will also be equal to the transformation rate of products of the same pair of goods for all the firms of the fishing industry, also being equal to the price ratio between the two goods.*

The neoclassical welfare theory applied to natural resources (Randall, 1981; Hannesson, 1978; Schmid, 1978, 1989) considers several welfare approaches that have different distributional implications of costs and resulting benefits of alternative management strategies (Table 5.1).

Table 5.1. Welfare criteria applied to marine fisheries.

Welfare Criteria	Distributional Characteristic	Impact
Pareto Efficiency	Economic damage is permissible	Neutral for the less efficient fishers
Pareto Safety	Economic damage is not allowed	Neutral for all fishers
Maximum value of the social product	Permissible economic damage is allowed if the $\sum$ welfare > 0 and maximized	Neutral
Proportional parts	Absolute or relative economic damage between fishers is not allowed	Proportional
Maximum social welfare	Economic damage is allowed. Assumes the existence of a social indifference curve	Neutral

Pareto efficiency. This approach consists in eliminating the inefficient management solutions. It should be mentioned however, that more than one efficient solution could exist since any point of the Grand Utility Frontier (*GUF*) curve involves efficiency in: (a) resource allocation, (b) production, and (c) consumption (Randall, 1981: 111-118). Each point of the *GUF* curve is *Pareto efficient*, because it does not consider:

(i) The combinations of inputs that do not remain in the *production possibilities curve.*
(ii) The distribution of goods that don't remain in the consumption efficiency curve.
(iii) All the points that don't remain in the *GUF* curve.

The concept of **Pareto Efficiency** is therefore defined as a situation in which it is impossible to improve a fisher without simultaneously damaging another. In order to achieve this goal, all the possibilities of voluntary exchange that allow reallocating resources or redistributing goods in a more efficient manner, have been exhausted. However, inherent to each point of the *GUF* curve is an initial distribution of wealth. This indicates that the selection of a given fishery management strategy will involve value judgments by policy makers, since they will implicitly consider a given initial distribution of wealth. The efficiency approach permits economic damage: as total efficiency must be reached through exchange, an initial distribution of rights will affect the distribution of benefits and costs.

Pareto safety. This approach searches for improvements in the fishing sector, with the condition that the selected management strategy must increase the income of a group of fishers **without reducing** the income of others in the fishery. In welfare theory, this concept is defined as *Paretian improvement*, where economic damage is not permitted. However, a relative economic damage could exist, since although the reduction in the income of any fisher is not allowable, the relative distribution of the wealth could change.

Maximum value of social welfare. This approach allows for real economic damage inside the limits defined by the social indifference curve, since the optimum is located at its tangent point with the *GUF*. Even though there has been academic discussion concerning the impossibility of estimating a social indifference curve (Arrow, 1976), the general concept could be applied to fisheries in a qualitative way. Thus, economic damage is permitted only when there is **social agreement** in that the selected management strategy represents an improvement in the social welfare of the fishing sector as a whole.

Maximum value of the social product. This management approach is the basis of benefit-cost analysis, *i.e.*, the management strategy with the greatest present value of the social product is selected. Economic damage is permissible when the sum of the economic rents obtained by the winners is highest and exceeds the losses of fishers that did not obtain economic rent. The analytic principles are similar to those of the previous approach, but in this case the indifference curve is assumed as a straight line with slope -1. The optimum solution, *i.e.*, the management strategy to be selected, is the tangent of the indifference curve with the *GUF* curve. A slope –1 in the indifference curve means the absence of distributional weights for society.

Proportional constant parts. This approach defines a management strategy as an improvement that results in proportional increments in fishers incomes. Therefore, **all fishers** are benefited from the new management strategy in proportion to their initial income. Economic damage is not allowed. However, the distribution of the absolute amount of rent generated by the fishery is not the same for each fisher, but is in proportion to the relative rent previous to the implementation of the new management strategy.

The above mentioned approaches could be combined in management plans, and policy-makers should make explicit the *distributional value judgments* inherent to each approach.

Intergenerational equity approach

The concept of intergenerational equity means that future generations have the same opportunities as current ones of using (with or without consumption) fishing resources. Thus, exploitation rates will determine the availability of a given stock for future generations. If this approach is considered relevant for the policy maker, a dynamic analysis will be needed to determine which will be the magnitude of the spatio-temporal allocation of fishing effort that should allow to sustain resource availability over time.

Other management approaches

Generation of employment and foreign exchange, as well as the contribution of food to coastal countries, could constitute relevant approaches for fisheries management. Although the generation of employment could be inefficient in economic terms, it could be important in order to achieve political and social stability.

Administrative and politic feasibility. Fishery regulations need administrative feasibility, because their implementation is time consuming (resource monitoring and control). However, the most important issue relates to enforcement costs (see Chapter 1), and thus fishers should participate, understand and share the regulatory measures imposed. The activity of the fishery also needs to be monitored, since different regulations will imply different strategies for monitoring and data collection from primary and secondary sources of information.

When a management strategy is evaluated, policy makers usually consider its political feasibility, because of the possible repercussions on their own political credibility. They could weight the repercussions of different management measures in a bio-socio-economic framework, including the risk of stock overexploitation, potential conflicts between different groups of fishers, or even international conflicts with coastal contiguous States in case of shared resources. The recognition of political costs is a factor that could influence a policy maker when considering adopting a management measure.

5.2. Management strategies

A fishery management plan can be carried out through allocation of property rights, regulation of catch composition, regulation of the catch size and the adoption of extension fishing programs (Anderson, 1977; Pearse, 1980; Seijo, 1986).

Property regimes and allocation of property rights

Four different property regimes (state, private, common and open access) were discussed in Chapter 1 and thus will not considered in detail here. However, some specific aspects deserve more consideration in the context of the present Chapter.

Under open access, many developed fisheries of the world were overexploited, overcapitalized, and generated externalities. As a result, coastal States implemented different approaches to allocating property rights as mentioned in Chapter 1. Under state property conditions, the management agency establishes the norms of use and access to the fish stock. Rights allocation includes the regulation of the amount and composition of the catch. Under a common property regime, exclusive rights are given to groups of fishers (having the right to exclude others), which we generally organized into cooperatives or fishing communities (Berkes, 1989; Ostrom, 1990; Seijo, 1993). Finally, the allocation of private property rights has been explored since the 80's by setting Individual Transferable Quotas (*ITQ's*: see Morgan, 1997).

Fishing rights could be allocated to fishers in a "community-based" context, using species or fishing areas as criteria for setting quotas/privileges (Defeo, 1989; Castilla, 1994). This implies the decision to exclude others, and thus the explicit definition of differential access to a specific fishing area or stock. These individuals or organizations acquire responsibility, although not exclusive, over the exploitation rates of the resource, defining their own norms of use (Acheson & Reidman, 1982; Seijo & Fuentes, 1989). The number of vessels and fishers should be fixed not only as a function of the perceived economic benefits, but also considering sustainable biomass and production levels. This management regime could be efficiently applied to sedentary species in a regional context. Defeo (1989, 1996) and Castilla (1994) documented successful community-based examples in Uruguayan and Chilean small-scale benthic shellfisheries. The execution of large-scale experiments in connection with artisanal fishers communities allowed specific hypotheses to be listed about natural re-stocking of overexploited invertebrates, including the economical viability of this operation. Even though fishermen's communities took care of their traditional fishing grounds by preventing illegal fishing, and allowed invertebrate stocks to rebuild, in both cases the State implemented an effective monitoring system to evaluate resource status over time.

Each form of right allocation has inherent value judgments that should be explicitly made, also recognizing the corresponding advantages and limitations (Pearse, 1980; Young, 1981; Schmid, 1987).

Regulation of catch composition

Regulation of catch composition is generally directed at protecting a critical phase of the life cycle of a species. This strategy could be carried out by: (a) closed seasons, mainly in spawning periods; (b) closing nursery areas to protect the spawning stock, or grounds with important occurrence of juveniles; (c) controlling gear selectivity; (d) restricting certain fishing gears, explosives and poisons; and (e) setting a minimum harvestable size. The response of the stock to alternative regulations will depend on the biological characteristics of the stock.

Regulation of the amount of catch

Restricting fishing effort through the following criteria could regulate the amount of catch: (a) number of vessels; (b) fishing power; (c) spatial distribution of fishing intensity; and (d) effective fishing time. The main regulation instruments are: (1) vessels quotas by fishing gear; (2) catch quotas by season and/or locality; (3) taxes and subsidies; (4) closed areas, marine refugia or marine protected areas; (5) changes in the duration of a closed season; and (6) spatio-temporal restrictions in the use of a fishing gear.

The standard procedure for limiting fishing effort has been to define catch quotas based on a reference point, the total allowable catch, according to abundance estimates. This could be difficult in practice, due to population fluctuations, catch flows and fishing power variations over time. It is also difficult to define how to allocate catches among fishers or even between countries (shared resource).

Allocation of quotas by type of vessel is also complicated when heterogeneous fishing fleets operate over the same stock. In these cases, we require to know the corresponding fishing power, the frequency distribution of fishing days, the effective fishing time per day and the fishing gear(s) used. Effort standardization is difficult in cases where different fishing methods or types of vessels are used to exploit a single or multiple stock. Moreover, since many fisheries have shown increasing fishing power in the absence of major changes in equipment, the skill of the skipper and the crew must be integrated to analyze and standardize the fishing power of individual vessels. In this context, the generalized linear model provides a powerful method for examining the effects of vessels, areas, gears and fishers's skill on the fishing power (Hilborn & Walters, 1992).

By mid 80's, the use of privatization management schemes began. In order to promote an optimal use of marine resources, some coastal countries like New Zealand, United States, Norway, and Chile, allocated property rights to individual fishers through Individual Transferable Quotas (*ITQ's*) (Morgan, 1997). Under an *ITQ* system, individual fishers, fishing companies and/or processing plants, have exclusive rights over a percentage of the annual catch quota. The owners of *ITQ's* carry out commercial transactions between them, adjusting their production flows to satisfy the total quota. Equilibrium rents and prices are generated, and the benefits of quota exchange are permitted to accumulate to users. As a result, the fishing industry is reorganized on a basis of efficiency, since the most efficient firms buy *ITQ's* from firms with greater costs. However, Squires *et al.* (1995) stated that: (i) the potential rents and improvements in surveillance efficiency should be enough to guarantee an *ITQ's* program, and (ii) the possibility of concentration of the fishing structure exists, thus affecting distribution of wealth and promoting monopolies (see also Anderson 1994, 1995). Hannesson (1993) pointed out that *ITQ's* could lead to efficient utilization of fish stocks. He discussed different ways of allocating quotas (*e.g.,* as fixed quantities or shares in the total allowable catch), and also the socio-economic implications derived from *ITQ's* at two levels: (a) when individual quotas are allocated; and (b) when individual quotas are exchanged. Even though he defined *ITQ's* as "particularly promising as an incentive-compatible and cost-efficient system of management", he highlighted that high control and enforcement costs are the major drawbacks that could make *ITQ's* an ineffective management method (see Hannesson, 1993 for details).

Restriction of licenses will limit vessel entry to the fishery. As in the previous case, the problem arises in defining to whom the licenses are granted and how many types of licenses are necessary when different types of vessels exist. Moreover, the limitation of the number of licenses must be based on a continuous monitoring of catches and of the state of the resource, which implies high information costs. Surveillance costs will also tend to increase, since fishers to whom the licenses were not granted could try to fish illegally.

Another approach to limiting the amount of fishing effort is through taxes and subsidies, which will affect fixed and variable costs. Subsidies could be used in low-income communities, thus increasing the amount of effort exerted. Subsidies stimulate the participation in the fishing activity and their suppression could imply effort reduction and unemployment, which is not desirable from a normative, political and social point of view (Panayotou, 1983). On the other hand, taxes tend to discourage users to introduce new vessels to the fishery.

The introduction of new technologies will increase fishing power. Competition among fishers could stimulate the introduction of technologies, which increases catch efficiency and the risks of stock overexploitation. Thus, some regulation schemes prohibit the use of gears with a strong impact on stocks (Anderson, 1980).

Extension programs and environmental education

The previous measures need complementary extension programs regarding the intelligent use of marine resources. For this reason, research results must be transferred to fisheries communities through education programs, technical bulletins and audio-visual material.

5.3. Multiple criteria optimization approach for fisheries management

Management of marine fisheries is significantly complicated by the fact that usually there are more than one set of criteria of relevance in evaluating fishery performance. The problem is not just one of maximizing the economic rent generated by fishery (given certain inter-temporal preferences), but also of sustaining biomass of target and incidental (usually threatened) species above certain levels, and perhaps of maximizing food production, coastal employment, and export earnings. In this type of problem, decision-makers must make trade-offs between conflicting criteria.Then, the goal of the optimization process must be to assist in ensuring that the best possible trade-offs are made for a given fishery management problem. This involves seeking so-called "Pareto optimal solutions" to multiple criterion optimization problems. A Pareto optimal solution in this context, has the property that one decision-making criterion cannot be improved by a decision without making the fishery performance worse off with respect to at least one other resource management criterion (Hannesson, 1978; Mendelssohn, 1979).

Optimal control theory has been applied to fisheries to identify the level of fishing effort that maximizes the net present value of economic rent in a variety of fishery contexts (Clark, 1985; Cohen, 1987; Hilborn & Walters, 1987). Multi-criteria and/or non-linear optimization models have seldom been used in fishery management (Garrod & Shepherd, 1981; Kennedy & Watkins, 1986; Onal *et al.*, 1991). Recently, hybrid simulation-optimization models have been developed for the estimation of optimal management strategies of a sequential fishery (Díaz de León & Seijo, 1992) and for a fishery with techno-ecological interdependencies (Seijo *et al.* 1994c). The approach combined multi-criteria and non-linear optimization modeling in a Pareto-optimal manner. The procedure allowed working with multiple input-outputs, time delays, non-linear functions and the natural trade-offs during the estimation process. The strategy involves minimizing with respect to a single criterion, namely, the maximum deviation of all fishery performance variables with respect to specific targets assigned for each of them (Osyczka, 1984, Manetsch, 1985). The method works at the beginning with the criteria with the largest goal deviation until it no longer has the largest target deviation. Then, it proceeds to improve the next management criterion which at that point experience the worse goal deviation, and so on. The method stops when all the fishery performance criteria experiences essentially the same goal deviations. It has been shown to be a useful decision-making aid when explicit manager objectives are available.

M-OPTSIM (Manetsch, 1986) is an optimization package that uses the non-linear optimization method COMPLEX (Box, 1965). It can be applied to resolve highly complex optimization problems (*e.g.* optimization of management strategies in multispecific fisheries) with difficult-to-find global optimal solutions. The Box method has proven to be an effective way to find the neighborhood of the global optimum.

The Multi-Criteria Objective Function

Given a dynamic model built for a fishery (as the one described in the previous Chapters), the block diagram for the multi-criteria optimization problem is based on:

$$\overline{E_\mu}(T) = (\overline{v_\mu}, T) \qquad \textbf{(5.1)}$$

where:

$\overline{E}_\mu\ (T)$ is the vector of values for the multi-criteria function corresponding to the management option μ, assessed in the time horizon $(0,\ T)$ selected to evaluate alternative management options; and $\overline{\upsilon}_\mu$ is a decision parameter vector corresponding to the management option μ. The dynamic model is then operated in optimization mode (Figure 5.1).

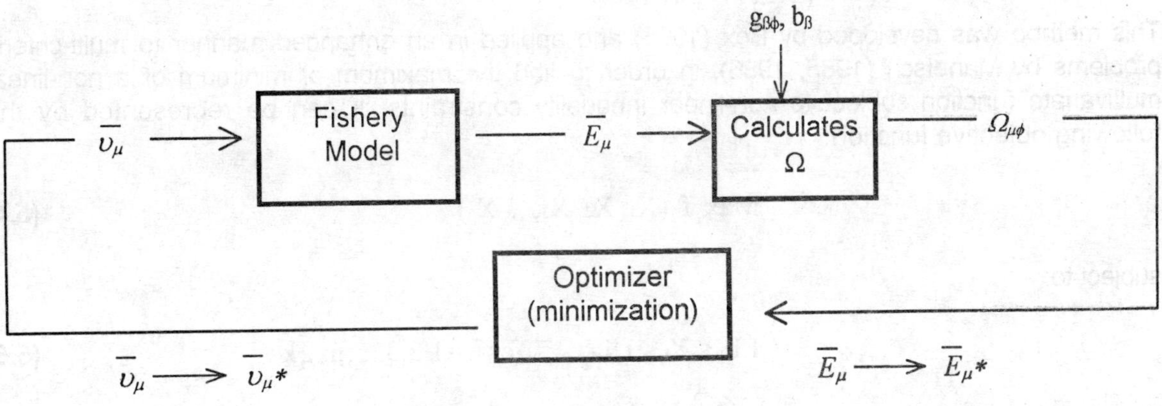

Figure 5.1 Conceptual block diagram for multi-criteria optimization of fisheries.

In Figure 5.1, $\Omega_{\mu\phi}$ could be expressed as follows:

$$\Omega_{\mu\phi} = \text{MIN}[\underset{\beta}{\text{MAX}}[\Omega_{\beta\mu\phi}]] \tag{5.2}$$

where $\Omega_{\beta\mu\phi}$ is the normalized deviation of the criterion value β with regard to the management option μ and goal set ϕ, and is expressed as follows:

$$\Omega_{\beta\mu\phi} = \frac{g_{\beta\phi} - E_{\beta\mu}}{|b_\beta|\, sgn(g_{\beta\phi} - b_\beta)} \tag{5.3}$$

where $g_{\beta\phi}$ is the target for the criterion β of the goal set ϕ; $E_{\beta\mu}$ is the value of the criterion β for the management strategy μ; and b_β is the base run value of β.

Finally, $\bar{\upsilon}_\mu*$ in Fig. 5.1 is the parameter vector for optimal control of the fishery, *i.e.*, the vector that specifies the optimal combination of fishery management instruments; and $\bar{E}_\mu*$ is the vector of optimal values for the multiple criteria function used to evaluate fishery performance. The *sgn* () function changes the sign of $\Omega_{\beta\mu\phi}$ for those goals which are less than the "base" values. In this way, $\Omega_{\beta\mu\phi}$ values related to different variables, strategies and goal sets could be compared.

The iterative procedure finds the largest deviation and minimizes it, operating on all criteria until no significant improvement can be made in the one with the largest goal deviation. For this reason, the "min-max" method tends to find optimal Pareto solutions to the multi-criteria optimization problem. The problem with this approach is the possibility of obtaining multiple solutions, some *Pareto inferior* to others. To cope with this, it is necessary to use a random search procedure, such as the one employed in the "Complex" method of Box (1965), that allows one to find the global optimum solution.

The "Complex" optimization method for non-linear functions with multiple criteria

This method was developed by Box (1965) and applied in an enhanced manner to multi-criteria problems by Manetsch (1985, 1986), in order to find the maximum or minimum of a non-linear multivariate function subject to non-linear inequality constraints. It can be represented by the following objective function:

$$\text{Max } f(X_1, X_2, X_3, \ldots, X_n) \tag{5.4}$$

subject to:

$$LL_i \leq X_i \leq UL_i \qquad \text{for } i = 1,2,3,\ldots,n\ldots,k \tag{5.5}$$

The implicit variables $X_{n+1},\ldots, X_k$ are dependent functions of the independent explicit variables $X_1, X_2, X_3,\ldots, X_n$, and the superior and inferior restrictions LL_i and UL_i could be either constants or independent variable functions. The method involves a sequential search procedure that attempts to find global optimum solutions, starting from an initial group of points randomly distributed within the feasible region. Each group of data corresponds to a vertex of a geometrical figure or "Complex" generated in the *n* dimension searching space. Associated with each vertex is a function value (calculated from a simulation model). The procedure converges toward a global optimum (Manetsch, 1985).

This method has been applied in marine fisheries to contend with management problems in which the resulting dynamic of the technological and ecological interdependencies means that the consideration of multiple criteria in the regulation process is a highly complex task (Díaz de León & Seijo, 1992; Seijo *et al.*, 1994c).

6. Spatial Bioeconomic Models

Models developed in Chapters 2 and 5 satisfy the dynamic pool assumption and thus homogeneity in the spatial distribution of the stock and fishing effort exerted (*e.g.* pelagic species). In sedentary resources (*e.g.,* mollusks), the above assumption is not always valid for the following reasons (see Hancock, 1973; Caddy, 1975; Orensanz & Jamieson, 1998):

(1) Populations are patchily distributed (Elliot, 1977).

(2) The low or null mobility precludes species redistribution over a fishing ground, by filling gaps in patches resulting from a sequential distribution pattern produced by the heterogeneous allocation of fishing effort (Hancock, 1979; Caddy, 1989a, b; Conan, 1984; Orensanz *et al.*, 1991). Thus, *CPUE cannot be used* as an unbiased index of abundance.

(3) Growth, mortality and recruitment parameters are extremely dependent on environmental conditions even between small distances (Orensanz, 1986; Defeo, 1993a).

Two alternative approaches seem to be appropriate:

1) To relax the assumption of spatial homogeneity of stock distribution. Thus, extensive fishing grounds with variability in environmental conditions and related abundance heterogeneity, growth and mortality patterns, can be divided into smaller areas that can be considered as independent units (Caddy, 1975; 1989a; b; Hall, 1983; Sluczanowski, 1984; 1986). Hence, for a stock showing a continuous geographic range of population characteristics, a useful approach is to consider it as composed of several discrete subpopulations which can be studied independently, and the predictions integrated afterwards (Seijo *et al.*, 1994b, c).

2) To develop a comprehensive approach, integrating effects of different environmental regimes on the spatial structure of the population, spatial heterogeneity of fishing effort, biological interactions, and the implications of economic factors and human attitudes (behavior of resource managers and users) (Seijo & Defeo, 1994a; Seijo *et al.*, 1994c). In view of the uncertainty involved in the above factors (Lewis, 1982; Anderson, 1984; Sissenwine, 1984a, b; Seijo, 1987), it is preferable to build stochastic models instead of deterministic ones, in which point predictions are replaced by probability functions (Botsford, 1986; Seijo, 1986; Fogarty, 1989; Seijo & Defeo, 1994a; Seijo *et al.*, 1994b).

Studies on fishing effort dynamics have been focused on long-term decisions of fishers, emphasizing the estimation of rates of entry and exit to the fishery and the characterization of general patterns of allocation of fishing intensity (Smith, 1969; Clark, 1976; Mangel & Clark, 1983; Emerson & Anderson, 1989). However, it is in the short-term that fishers make their spatial decisions: after deciding to go fishing and selecting the target species they decide where to fish (Hilborn & Ledbetter, 1979; Bockstael & Opaluch, 1983; Defeo *et al.*, 1991; Eales & Wilen, 1986). The latter decisions are of utmost importance, because, in contrast with traditional views which focus on excess of fleet capitalization, dissipation of economic rent can arise primarily as a result of today's excess of fishermen's movements in response to yesterday's spatial catch rate variations.

In this Chapter, spatial considerations in modelling fisheries are introduced, notably the distance from ports to fishing grounds, in order to further understand short-run decision-making of fishers in their allocation of fishing intensity. We also add a degree of complexity in the interdependencies discussed in Chapter 3, incorporating the spatial dimension in the analysis, with special reference to fisheries where the dynamic pool assumption is not satisfied.

6.1. Spatial allocation of fishing intensity

Modelling the spatial dynamics of fisheries in the short-term allows us to better understand the intertemporal allocation behavior of fishing effort and thus to develop adequate management strategies. Some strategies of spatial allocation of effort have been identified:

(i) **Proportional** allocation according to the spatial abundance of the resource (Caddy, 1975).
(ii) **Sequential** allocation to those patches of greatest abundance (Hilborn & Walters, 1987).
(iii) **Random search** (Hilborn & Walters, 1987).
(iv) **Free distribution** of allocation of fishing intensity (Gillis *et al.,* 1993).
(v) **Proportional allocation to** (Defeo *et al.,* 1991; Seijo *et al.,* 1994b):

- The quasi rent of variable costs (including transfer costs resulting from moving from port to alternative fishing grounds).
- The *friction of distance*, *i.e.,* non-monetary costs associated to distance.
- The probability of finding the target species at profitable levels.

With the above considerations in mind, we present two models developed by Seijo *et al.* (1994b), with different degree of complexity in spatial resolution and requirement of bioeconomic information.

6.2. Short-run spatial dynamics: ALLOC model

ALLOC is a short-run bioeconomic model that represents interdependencies between two fleet types (*e.g.* artisanal and mechanized/industrial) coming from different ports of origin that capture the same target species in alternative fishing grounds (Seijo *et al.*, 1994b).

Spatial and temporal dimensions are incorporated in this discrete dynamic model by specifying: (1) *CPUE*'s by fishing grounds; (2) distances from ports to different fishing grounds; and (3) a function that determines the short-run spatial allocation of fishing intensity. The latter is modelled in **ALLOC** as a function of the distances from ports to alternative fishing grounds, the net revenues perceived in the previous trips, and the probability of finding the target species in each ground at profitable levels.

Spatial allocation of fishing intensity

The spatial dynamic allocation of fishing intensity (*i.e.*, effective effort per unit of area, *sensu* Gulland, 1983: 44) of vessels type *m* from port *h* among fishing grounds *k* in time *t* ($f_{khm}(t)$) is given by:

$$f_{khm}(t) = SAE_{khm}(t) DAYS \cdot V_{hm}(t) \tag{6.1}$$

where $SAE_{khm}(t)$ is a (0,1) optimum spatial distribution of fishing vessels; *DAYS* is the average number of effective fishing days per month; and $V_{hm}(t)$ is the number of vessels type *m* of port *h* which seasonally allocate their fishing effort to the target species. $SAE_{ipm}(t)$ is estimated by:

$$SAE_{khm}(t) = \frac{\dfrac{P_k quasi\pi_{khm}(t)}{D_{kh}^{\phi m}}}{\sum_k \left(\dfrac{P_k quasi\pi_{khm}(t)}{D_{kh}^{\phi m}} \right)} \tag{6.2}$$

where P_k is the probability of finding the target species at profitable levels in alternative fishing grounds *k*; $quasi\pi_{khm}(t)$ is the quasi rent of variable costs received by the average vessel type *m* from port *h* in ground *k* in time *t*; D_{kh} is the distance to fishing ground *k* from port *h*; and ϕ_m is a weighing factor called *friction of distance* for vessel type *m*. P_k can be estimated by the ratio between total fishing trips per ground and the number of trips where the target species was found at profitable levels, *i.e.*, for those *CPUE* that generated net revenues greater than or equal to variable costs of fishing effort.

Distance to fishing grounds from different ports of origin

Additional to the *transfer costs* from the port of origin to alternative fishing grounds, one element considered in this model as a key explanatory factor for the spatial behavior of fleets is the *friction of distance* (Isard & Liossatos, 1979, Seijo *et al.*, 1994b). Artisanal boats with limited autonomy are assumed to give substantial weight to non monetary costs derived from *e.g.*, insecurity associated with fishing far away from port, as well as other environmental and cultural factors that assign non-monetary costs to distance. Thus, **ALLOC** implicitly incorporates in $D_{kh}^{\phi m}$ all those non-monetary factors associated with distance. The weight of this parameter for a specific fleet type *m*, is given by the power to which distance is raised ($D_{kh}^{\phi m}$ in equation 6.2).

Quasi rent of variable costs by fleet type from different ports of origin

To observe the short-term fleet performance, an estimation of the quasi rent received by an average vessel type *m* from port *h* is needed:

$$quasi\pi_{khm}(t) = TR_{khm}(t) - VC_{khm}(t) \tag{6.3}$$

where $TR_{khm}(t)$ are the daily total revenues received by vessel type *m* from port *h* by harvesting in fishing ground *k* in time *t*; and $VC_{khm}(t)$ are the variable costs of fishing effort incurred by vessel type *m* by fishing one day in ground *k* in time *t*.

$VC_{khm}(t)$ are estimated considering: (a) *transfer cost* (as a function of distance) defined as the product of D_{Kh} and the average cost of oil and gas per km traveled (θ) ; and (b) the value of the proportion of the catch (ϖ) assigned to the crew as labor payment. Other variable costs (*e.g.*, bait, gear maintenance and repair) are pooled together in a parameter called OVC_m:

$$VC_{khm}(t) = \varpi q_m B_k(t) + \theta D_{kh} + OVC_m \quad \textbf{(6.4)}$$

In the short-run, vessels will remain in the fishery if $TR_{khm}(t) \geq VC_{khm}(t)$, *i.e.*, the quasi rent of variable costs ≥ 0. Considering the $SAE_{khm}(t)$ function, at least four types of distributions that account for spatial variations in fishing intensity can be described (Table 6.1):

(i) ***Case 1: artisanal littoral fisheries.*** When the distance is irrelevant in terms of transfer costs from port to alternative grounds (θ=0) and the friction of distance is zero (ϕ=0), *i.e.*, there are not non-monetary costs to fishing the different grounds, and the same probability of finding the species at profitable levels exists ($P_1=P_2=...=P_k$, where k = $1..n$), the resulting $SAE_{khm}(t)$ distribution is proportional to the spatial variations in stock abundance.

(ii) ***Case 2: fisheries in protected coastal zones.*** Where transfer distances to alternative grounds from port are relevant ($\theta > 0$), but non-monetary costs are negligible because of the easy operation and navigability in protected fishing grounds ($\phi = 0$), and there is the same probability of finding the species at profitable levels ($P_1=P_2=...=P_i$, where i = $1..n$), the $SAE_{khm}(t)$ distribution is then proportional to spatial variations in the quasi-rent of variable costs.

(iii) ***Case 3: fisheries in exposed coastal zones.*** When θ>0, the friction of distance is substantial (ϕ>0), and $P_1=P_2=...=P_k$, the $SAE_{khm}(t)$ distribution is proportional to the spatial distribution of the quasi rent and inversely related to the friction of distance from port to the alternative grounds.

(iv) ***Case 4: fisheries with high information costs.*** When transfer distances from port to alternative grounds are relevant in monetary terms (D>0 y θ>0), friction of distance (ϕ>0) occurs, and there is heterogeneous probability of finding the resource at profitable levels ($P_1 \neq P_2 \neq ... \neq P_k$), the distribution of $SAE_{khm}(t)$ is proportional to the spatial distribution of the quasi rent and to the probability of finding the resource at profitable levels, and inversely related to the friction of distance from port to alternative fishing grounds.

Table 6.1. Properties of the *SAE* model.

CASES	Monetary cost of distance *D*	Friction of distance (ϕ)	Probability of finding the resource (*P*)	Expected distribution
Case 1	$D_1=D_2=...=D_k$ $\theta=0$	$\phi=0$	$P_1=P_2=...=P_k$	Proportional to the abundance
Case 2	$D_1\neq D_2\neq...\neq D_k$ $\theta>0$	$\phi=0$	$P_1=P_2=...=P_k$	Proportional to the quasi rent
Case 3	$D_1\neq D_2\neq...\neq D_k$ $\theta>0$	$\phi>0$	$P_1=P_2=...=P_k$	Proportional to the quasi rent and $1/D^{\phi}$
Case 4	$D_1\neq D_2\neq...\neq D_k$ $\theta>0$	$\phi>0$	$P_1\neq P_2\neq...\neq P_k$	Proportional to the quasi rent, $1/D^{\phi}$ and P_k

Spatial variations in net revenues

The cumulative economic rent received by vessel type *m* from port *h* over the fishing season is estimated by:

$$\pi_{khm}(t+DT)=\pi_{khm}(t)+\int_{t}^{t+DT}(TR_{khm}(\tau)-TC_{khm}(\tau))d\tau \qquad \textbf{(6.5)}$$

where $TR_{khm}(t)$ are the total revenues received by vessel type *m* from port *p* by harvesting in fishing ground *k*, in time *t*; and $TC_{khm}(t)$ are the total costs of fishing effort incurred by the fleet type *m* by fishing in ground *k* in time *t*.

$TR_{khm}(t)$ and $TC_{khm}(t)$ are estimated respectively as:

$$TR_{khm}(t)=(q_m B_k(t)Ptar+Cinc\ Pinc)\,f_{khm}(t) \qquad \textbf{(6.6)}$$

$$TC_{khm}(t)=FC_m V_{hm}+VC_{khm}(t)\,f_{khm}(t) \qquad \textbf{(6.7)}$$

where: *Ptar* and *Pinc* are, respectively, the average price paid per kg of target and incidental species; *Cinc* is the average incidental catch per fishing trip of vessel *m*; q_m is the catchability coefficient of vessel type *m*; $B_k(t)$ is the biomass of the target species in fishing ground *k* in time *t*; FC_m is the daily fixed cost for vessel type *m*; and V_{hm} is the number of vessels *m* from port *h*. Fixed costs include interest payments from borrowed capital to buy a boat, engine and gear, their depreciation, administration and insurance costs, and the opportunity cost of capital.

The dynamic catch rate is estimated as:

$$Y_{khm}(t)=(q_m B_k(t)+RV_{khm}(t))\,f_{khm}(t) \qquad \textbf{(6.8)}$$

where the random variable $RV_{khm}(t)$ is generated with an exponentially autocorrelated probability density function, using the observed variance of daily catch for vessels type *m* when fishing in ground *k*. This variable accounts for catch variability not explained by variations in *q*, *B* and *f* in each fishing ground. It is exponentially autocorrelated to represent the fact that random catch variations at one day are not independent of previous values: (a) today's catch is dependent to a certain extent of yesterday's catch; (b) selection of fishing ground is partially dependent on previously selected grounds; (c) environmental factors affecting resource abundance tend also to be dependent on previous values. This variable is generated by subroutine **EXACOR** (Manetsch, 1986), which uses an uniformly distributed random variable between 0 and 1, that is further transformed to the selected probability density function. Other probability density functions can be used to generate random variables, by employing the inverse transformation method or even numerical methods, depending on whether the probability density function can be integrated analytically to obtain the cumulative distribution function or not (Gottfried, 1984).

Spatial *CPUE*

The catch per unit of effort of vessel type *m* in ground *k* in time *t* ($CPUE_{km}(t)$) is estimated by:

$$CPUE_{km}(t) = q_m B_k(t) \tag{6.9}$$

Biomass for each fishing ground $B_k(t)$ is estimated by spatially disaggregating the logistic function:

$$B_k(t+DT) = B_k(t) + \int_t^{t+DT} \left[r_k B_k(\tau)\left(1 - \frac{B_k(\tau)}{Bmax_k}\right)\right] - \sum_{hm} Y_{khm}(\tau))dt \tag{6.10}$$

where r_k and *Bmax*, are respectively, the intrinsic growth rate and the maximum biomass in ground *k*.

Fleet dynamics

A time lag frequency distribution representing the rate at which small-scale fishing fleets enter the seasonal fishery or shift from one fishery to another, is frequently observed (Seijo *et al.*, 1987). Hence, time lags in the short-run dynamics of fishing fleets are incorporated in **ALLOC** to relax the assumption that every boat that eventually will fish for the seasonal target species, will enter the fishery exactly the first day of the season. This aspect is incorporated through the distributed DELAY model (Manetsch, 1976) based on the Erlang (Gamma) probability density function (Seijo, 1987). Thus, the seasonal dynamics of vessel type *m* from different ports ($V_{hm}(t)$) can be described by a distributed delay function of order *g* by the following set of differential equations (see also Chapters 2 and 4):

(6.11)

$$\frac{d\gamma_1}{dt} = \frac{g}{DEL_m}(V_{hm}(t) - \gamma_1(t))$$

$$\frac{d\gamma_2}{dt} = \frac{g}{DEL_m}(\gamma_1(t) - \gamma_2(t))$$

$$\frac{d\gamma_g}{dt} = \frac{g}{DEL_m}(\gamma_{g-1} - \gamma_g(t))$$

where V_{hm} is the input to the delay process (number of vessels from port *h* which will allocate their fishing effort to target species); $\gamma t_g(t)$ is the output of the delay process (number of small-scale boats entering the fishery along the season); $\gamma_1(t)$, $\gamma_2(t)$,..., $\gamma_{g-1}(t)$ are intermediate rates of the delay; *DEL* is the expected time of entry of vessels to the fishery; and *g* is the order of the delay. The parameter *g* specifies the member of the Gamma family of probability density functions.

The cumulative spatial allocation of fishing intensity along the fishing season of fleets *m* from port *h* in ground *k* ($fa_{khm}(t)$) is given by:

$$fa_{hm}(t+DT) = fa_{khm}(t) + \int_{t}^{t+DT} SAE_{khm}(\tau)\, DAYS\ \ V_{hm}(\tau)\, d\tau \qquad \textbf{(6.12)}$$

Model assumptions

(i) The spatial allocation of fishing intensity among alternative fishing grounds is a function of the probability of finding the target species, the net revenues obtained from different fishing grounds in previous trips, and the distances to alternative fishing grounds from different ports of origin.

(ii) *CPUE* is a function of *q* and the resource biomass in each fishing ground over time, and will tend to decrease as fishing intensity and the corresponding exploitation rate (*sensu* Gulland, 1983) increase at a higher rate than the natural biomass growth rate in each site.

(iii) There is no cross migration or immigration among fishing grounds.

(iv) Uncertainty in the spatial allocation of fishing effort over time is represented by random variables (0, VAR) with an exponentially autocorrelated probability density function.

(v) Fishers price-taking behavior (Clark, 1985) was assumed for prices of target species and incidental catch. This assumption could be relaxed if a robust time series of fish price, quantity harvested and real income of resource consumers were available.

(vii) Costs of inputs needed per fishing trip remains constant along the fishing season.

6.3. Short and long-run geographic bioeconomic dynamics: CHART model

When bioeconomic information is available, some of the assumptions made in **ALLOC** can be relaxed to achieve a better representation of the population dynamics and of the spatial resolution of the model. **CHART** is an age structured, dynamic spatial model that incorporates the main features of the **YRAREA** model (Caddy, 1975) with the short and long run dynamics of the fishing fleets in a bioeconomic and geographic context (Seijo *et al.*, 1994b).

Spatial specification of maximum biomass and recruitment

The initial population structure is estimated by the maximum observed *CPUE* on each ground ($CPUEmax_{kl}$), where *k* is the latitude and *l* the longitude. Maximum biomass in each geographic cell *kl* ($Bmax_{kl}$) is obtained by dividing $CPUEmax_{kl}$ by an average *q* per unit area. Recruitment over time can be specified as constant, dynamic, deterministic or stochastic. It involves a general stock-recruitment function built-in in addition to the upper bound imposed by the estimated maximum biomass of each cell of the geographic area. The model uses a Beverton-Holt stock-recruitment type of model (Beverton & Holt, 1957). For a given maximum recruitment (R_{max}), the number of recruits is estimated as follows:

$$R(t) = \frac{\sum_{kl} B_{kl}(t) R\max}{\frac{\sum_{kl} B\max_{kl}}{2} + \sum_{kl} B_{kl}(t)} + RN(t) \qquad \textbf{(6.13)}$$

where $B_{kl}(t)$ is the biomass in cell *kl*; and *RN(t)* is a (0, var) normally distributed random variable.

Spatial distribution of recruitment patches

Total number of recruits for each year is seasonally distributed through the use of a distributed delay function, which specifies the peak recruitment month and its period (in months) of occurrence. The spatial distribution of recruitment patches is generated by randomly selecting the recruitment patch center coordinates, and then calculating recruitment density out from patch center by using the bivariate normal distribution (Caddy, 1975):

$$R_{kl}(t) = \frac{NT(t)}{\sqrt{2\pi\sigma^2}} e^{(-x^2/2\sigma^2)} \qquad \textbf{(6.14)}$$

where: $R_{kl}(t)$ is the number of recruits located in the patch center of the cell *kl* in time *t*; *NT(t)* is the number of recruits to be distributed within each patch before biomass constraint (see Seijo *et al.*, 1994b); σ is the standard deviation of the patch density ($0 < \sigma < 1$), and *x* is the distance of unit area *kl* from patch center, estimated by:

$$x = \sqrt{[TSG(y-K)]^2 + [TTG(z-L)]^2} \qquad \textbf{(6.15)}$$

where *TSG* and *TTG* are, respectively, the length and width of the cell, estimated by a previously specified spatial resolution (*e.g.* degrees, minutes and seconds). Moreover:

i = 1, 2, 3,..., *SG*	and	*SG* = number of rows in the geographic grid.
j = 1, 2, 3,..., *TG*	and	*TG* = number of columns in the geographic grid.
y = SG/2	and	z = *TG/2*.

Spatial distribution of resource biomass

The biomass allocated in each cell *kl* is estimated by:

$$B_{kl}(t) = \sum_{j=1}^{mage} N_{jkl}(t) W_j \quad (6.16)$$

where $N_{jkl}(t)$ is the number of individuals at age j in site kl in time t and $mage$ is the maximum observed age. Average individual weight at age (W_j) is calculated by the von Bertalanffy growth equation and the corresponding length-weight relationship:

$$L_j = L_\infty(1 - e^{(-kp(j-t_0))}) \quad (6.17)$$

$$W_j = aL_j^{\ b} \quad (6.18)$$

where a and b are constants.

The spatio-temporal distribution of population structure ($N_{jkl}(t)$) is estimated by:

$$N_{jkl}(t+DT) = N_{jkl}(t) + \int_t^{t+DT} (S_{jkl-1}(\tau) N_{jkl-1} - N_{jkl}(\tau)) d\tau \quad (6.19)$$

where $S_{jkl}(t)$ corresponds to the finite survival rate at age k in site with coordinates kl in time t:

$$S_{jkl}(t) = \left[1 - (1 - e^{(-M + F_{jkl}(t))})\right] \quad (6.20)$$

where M is the instantaneous natural mortality rate and $F_{jkl}(t)$ is the age specific fishing mortality rate in site kl in time t, estimated by the product of the age-specific q_j by the intensity of fishing exerted in site kl in time t ($f_{kl}(t)$).

Spatial *CPUE*

CPUE in site kl in time t ($CPUE_{kl}(t)$) is estimated by:

$$CPUE_{kl}(t) = \sum_j (qua_j N_{jkl}(t)\ W_j) \quad (6.21)$$

where the age specific catchability per unit of area (qua_j) is estimated using the area swept equation of Baranov (1918) and the logistic selectivity curve (Sparre *et al.*, 1989):

$$qua_i = -\left[\ln\left(1 - \frac{\frac{pcap\ area\ SEL_j}{AREA}}{SG\ TG}\right)\right] \quad (6.22)$$

where: *pcap* is the probability of capture by the gear; *area* is the area swept per day; SEL_J is the age-specific gear retention (see Chapter 4); and *AREA* is the area occupied by the stock.

Short-run fleet dynamics: spatial allocation of fishing intensity

Short-run spatial allocation of fishing intensity (*e.g.* within the fishing season) is estimated as in **ALLOC**, with one modification: parameter P_K is substituted by the perceived risk of fishing on the fishing ground with coordinates *kl*.

Spatial allocation of fishing intensity of vessels from port *h* in site *kl* in time *t*, ($f_{klh}(t)$) is given by:

$$f_{klh}(t) = SAE_{klh}(t) DAYS\ V_h(t) \tag{6.23}$$

where: $V_p(t)$ is the number of vessels from port *h* that seasonally allocate their fishing effort to the target species; and $SAE_{klh}(t)$ is a (0,1) distribution of vessels of port *h* into sites with coordinates *kl*, in time *t*, which can be estimated as:

$$SAE_{klh}(t) = \frac{\dfrac{quasi\pi_{klh}(t)}{Risk_{kl} D_{klh}{}^{\phi}}}{\sum_{K} \left(\dfrac{quasi\pi_{klh}(t)}{Risk_{kl} D_{klh}{}^{\phi}} \right)} \tag{6.24}$$

where $Risk_{kl}$ is the perceived risk of fishing in alternative grounds *kl*. This parameter is specified in the model with a range of values [1 - 3], where 1 implies absence of risk and 2 - 3 indicates increasing risk levels. Catch and economic rent for each ground are estimated as in **ALLOC**.

Long-run fleet dynamics

The number of boats from port *h* present in the fishery over time (years), is modelled by spatially applying Smith (1969) equation:

$$\frac{dV_h}{dt} = \varphi_h \sum_{kl} \pi_{klh}(t) \tag{6.25}$$

where φ_h is a positive constant. Equation (6.25) states that in the long-run and under open access conditions, if the sum of net revenues obtained from all fishing grounds is: (i) positive, there will be entry to the fishery; (ii) negative, exit is expected to occur; and (iii) zero, the fishery is at bioeconomic equilibrium, and there will be no stimulus for exit/entry.

Model assumptions

(i) Recruitment does not occur at a single point in time, but within a period whose distribution is modelled by the distributed delay model.

(ii) Extension of patches is defined by the density variance of a bivariate normal distribution.

(iii) Migration, dispersal and movement are not considered.

(iv) Natural mortality is constant for all ages.

(v) Spatial allocation of fishing intensity is a function of ground-specific variations in the: (a) quasi-rent, (b) risk of fishing, and (c) distances from different ports.

(vi) Distances between ports and fishing grounds are estimated geographically without consideration of possible obstacles.

(vii) For the long-term fleet dynamics, an estimated time lag of 6 months is assumed for vessel entry/exit to the fishery, whereas in the short-run, the user is requested to provide the observed average time lag of entering the seasonal fishery.

(viii) Uncertainty of daily catches in each ground is modelled by an exponentially autocorrelated probability density function.

(ix) Price of target species and costs of fishing effort inputs are constant and exogenously determined.

The interested reader can conduct simulation experiments with these spatial models, which are contained in the package SPATIAL published by FAO (Seijo *et al.*, 1994b).

6.4. A spatial bioeconomic model for sedentary fisheries: the yellow clam *Mesodesma mactroides* of Uruguay, a study case

Seijo & Defeo (1994a) conducted a short and long run analysis of the yellow clam *Mesodesma mactroides* fishery of Uruguay. For this end, a dynamic, non-linear and stochastic model was built to represent the behavior of resource and fishers through time. The short term space-time distribution of fishing effort was represented as a function of the dynamic catch per unit effort in 4 alternative grounds, the distance from different localities, the perceived probability of finding the species at profitable levels, and the corresponding net revenues obtained in the previous fishing trip (see also Defeo *et al.*, 1991). The long-term dynamics of the fishery considered time lags in spawning, hatching and recruitment processes, as well as in fishermen's entry and exit to the fishery. The distributed delay model was applied for this purpose. A stock-dependent, overcompensatory (Ricker) function characterized the dynamics of the stock-recruitment relationship (Defeo, 1993a). Recruitment was modelled by using the distributed delay model (gamma function of order 3) in accordance with a recruitment period of 4 months. A dynamic and density-dependent natural mortality was estimated as a function of the initial density of recruits and salinity (which is substantially affected by the outflow of freshwater creeks) on each fishing ground. Effort dynamics in the long-run (number of fishers from locality *h* present in the fishery over time) was modelled by spatially applying the Smith (1969) equation and the distributed delay model (see Seijo & Defeo, 1994b). Price of species, opportunity costs of labor and operation costs were also included in the model.

Simulation experiments were conducted with three management strategies to observe the dynamic impact on performance variables. The following three policy vectors were simulated and compared with the base run representing the current management scheme (minimum size restriction of 50 mm, and 50 fishing licenses):

1) The current management scheme and a catch quota of 50 tonnes/year.

2) A minimum harvestable size of 43 mm (size at sexual maturity) and 150 fishing licenses.
3) Minimum size restriction of 50-mm and150 fishing licenses.

The resource

The model reproduced well the temporal variability in abundance of recruits (Fig. 6.1a) and adults (Fig. 6.1b), and was statistically validated. Adults markedly increased from 1988 on, as a result of a human exclusion experiment conducted between March 1987 and November 1989 (see Defeo, 1993a; 1996, 1998; Defeo & de Alava, 1995 for details). Recruitment was inhibited in 1989 and 1990, as a result of overcompensation due to high adult densities. This fact has important management connotations: simulation showed that, as a result of a prolonged closed season (more than 2 years), high adult density could inhibit recruitment success and hence the magnitude of the stock available for fishing two years later (see Fig. 6.2).

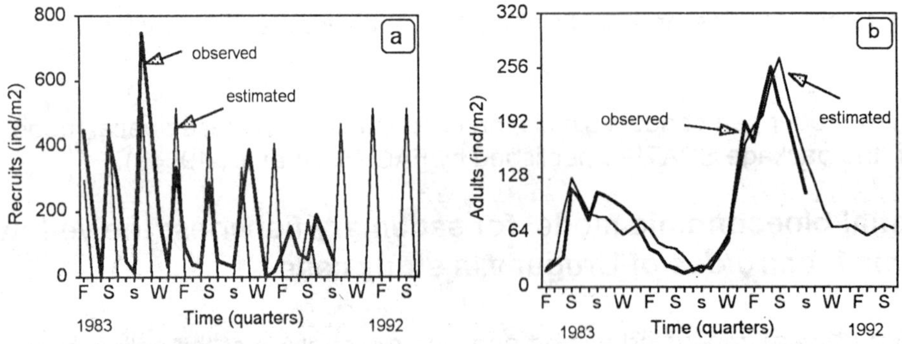

Figure 6.1 *Mesodesma mactroides*. Observed vs. estimated densities of (a) recruits and (b) adults.

The fishery

The fishery showed a strong seasonal component. The model (Fig. 6.2) adequately reproduced the marked increase in catch and fishing intensity during summer and spring. A decline in the demand for local market consumption and a reduced availability of the resource because of downward migration towards the infralittoral explained the diminished catches in autumn and winter (Defeo, 1989). The model also satisfactorily explained the marked spatial variability in effective fishing days, catches and fishing intensity (Fig. 6.3a; see also Defeo *et al.*, 1991), as well as spatial variations in the economic rent. Fishermen spatially allocated fishing effort proportionally to spatial variations in stock abundance, *i.e.,* the central zones 2 and 3, with greater stock abundance presented highest yield values (Fig. 6.3b) and fishing intensity. The model correctly represented variations within and between years. As a result of the above mentioned trends and the marked seasonality of the fishery, net revenues were also greater from the central grounds, peaking in spring and summer (see also Defeo *et al.*, 1991 for a detailed analysis).

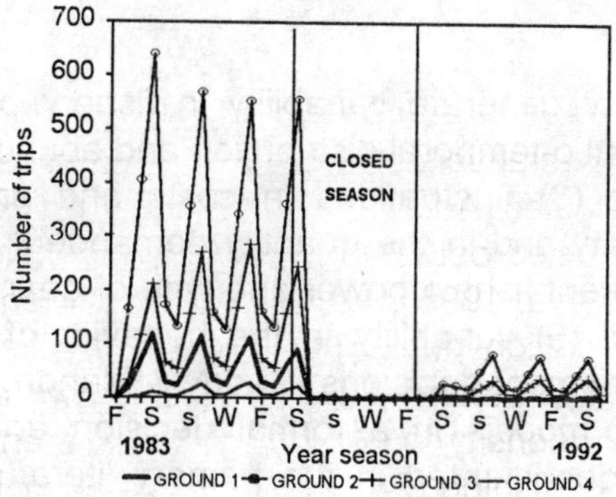

Figure 6.2 Seasonal variations in simulated fishing intensity by fishing ground from 1983 to 1992 for the yellow clam fishery of Uruguay.

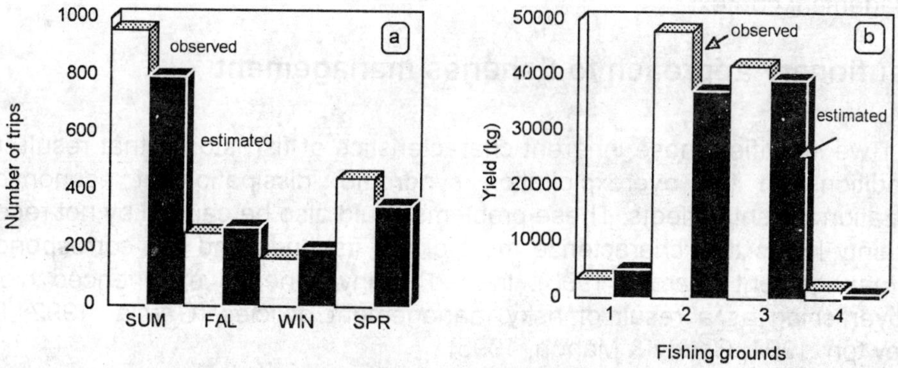

Figure 6.3 *Mesodesma mactroides*. Comparison of observed vs. simulated: (a) seasonal fishing effort; and (b) catches by fishing ground (summer 1985).

According to the results obtained, a spatial management scheme based upon a rotation of areas was proposed, taking into account periods of unequal demand for the product and temporal variations in stock accessibility and abundance. Because of relatively low total costs, the bioeconomic equilibrium is estimated at high levels of fishing effort, which in turn increases the risks of exhausting this highly vulnerable sedentary species.

7. Risk and Uncertainty: A Precautionary Approach

Several sources of uncertainty generate variability in fishery performance: (1) variability in abiotic factors affecting the spatio-temporal distribution and abundance of a stock; (2) effects of ecological interdependencies; (3) fluctuations in costs and product prices that determine changes in exploitation intensity and in the quantity demanded; (4) variations in fishing effort determined by fleets with different fishing power and type of gear, as well as by differential skill of the skipper and crew; and (5) variability in the behavior of policy makers due to value judgments when taking management decisions (Caddy & Mahon, 1995; FAO, 1995a, b). In this context, use of bioeconomic models in a formal decision analysis that explicitly includes uncertainty has been rarely documented in the primary literature. Because these uncertain events involve more than one possible outcome, bioeconomic evaluation of alternative management strategies requires the quantification of uncertainty and risk associated with the application of each strategy. In this Chapter, we summarize some types and sources of uncertainty and risk in fisheries. Moreover, some formal decision models directed to quantify the economic value of alternative management strategies are presented in a precautionary fishery management context.

7.1. Precautionary approach to fisheries management

In Chapter 1 we identified those inherent characteristics of fish stocks that result, under open access conditions, in the overexploitation syndrome, dissipation of economic rent and overcapitalization of fishing fleets. These problems could also be caused by not recognizing the high uncertainty levels that characterize most of the fisheries and the corresponding lack of caution in management (Garcia, 1996). Indeed, many fisheries experienced biological and economic overfishing as a result of risky management policies (Garcia, 1992; FAO, 1993; Garcia & Newton, 1994; Caddy & Mahon, 1995).

In June 1995, FAO and the Sweden Government organized in Lysekil (Sweden) a scientific consultation guided to establish a precautionary approach in the investigation and management of fishing resources (FAO, 1995a). The following definitions were adopted: (i) *risk* is the probability of occurrence of an undesirable event, (ii) *uncertainty* is the incompleteness of knowledge about the states or processes of nature, and (iii) *statistical uncertainty* is the stochasticity or error coming from several sources as described using statistical methodology.

7.2. Sources of uncertainty in fisheries

Hilborn & Peterman (1996) identify seven sources of uncertainty in fisheries stock assessment: (1) in the estimates of fish abundance; (2) in the structure of the mathematical model of the fishery; (3) when estimating model parameters; (4) in future environmental conditions; (5) in the response of users to regulations; (6) in future management objectives; and (7) in economical, political and social conditions (see Hilborn & Peterman, 1996, for details).

1. Uncertainty in abundance estimates. One of the main sources of error in abundance estimates can arise from incorrect or unreliable estimates of inputs used in stock assessment models. For example, stock estimates from *VPA* are based on time-invariant and mean values of *M* estimates made in the 1950s to 1980s (Caddy, 1996), when it is known that *M* strongly affects estimates of current abundance by this methodology (Lapointe *et al*., 1989). Moreover, many stock estimates are unreliable due to incomplete information concerning catch/effort data, which often results in biased abundance indexes (*CPUE*) and estimates of population structure significantly different from that observed. Variance and error structure of the entire data series might also be a source of uncertainty, and should be quantified (Schnute & Hilborn, 1993).

2. Uncertainty in model structure. Most of the models used in stock assessment are based on single-species population dynamics, although important ecological interdependencies have been recognized (see Chapter 3). Difficulties in data gathering and lack of robustness in abundance estimates make multispecies models quite unreliable.

Even for single-species models, uncertainty associated with model structure is often large and it is not usually reported. Results obtained by alternative models should be useful depending on which of them is most appropriate in a given situation. It may be also considered precautionary to fit several models, and for management purposes, emphasize the one that provides the most cautious approach. A detailed analysis of the basic assumptions of the model used and the estimation of uncertainty associated with the bioeconomic functions and equations fitted in a fishery model (see Chapter 4), should be a common practice to validate model structure and evaluate its performance (e.g. Caddy & Defeo, 1996). Several possible management options using the whole range of available bioeconomic models should ideally be systematically analyzed.

3. Uncertainty in estimation of model parameters. Although reporting the variance for bioeconomic parameters is attracting increasing attention by fisheries agencies, possible data biases and resulting estimates are rarely discussed and made explicit. Moreover, many key parameters used as inputs in stock assessment models, even in methods that purport to analyze yearly data as *VPA*, are assumed to be time-invariant, and variability around mean estimates are neither reported nor used to perform sensitivity analyses (Caddy, 1996). This tends to *underestimate uncertainty* in the parameters and, consequently, in the outcomes provided by the models.

4. Uncertainty in future environmental conditions. Changes in environmental conditions have an important impact on the abundance and spatio-temporal distribution of fish resources (Walters & Parma, 1996). In order to carry out dynamic forecasts of a stock, the prediction of environmental future conditions is required, especially for resources sensitive to an extreme degree to environmental changes. Three types of alternative assumptions are considered: (1) environmental constant conditions correspond to the average of the historical observations; (2) environmental conditions randomly vary conditions around the average, with a known probabilistic density function; and (3) environmental conditions show systematic patterns, *e.g.*, periodic or linear trends. In this context, random variability about past average conditions might be considered when modelling a fishery.

5. Uncertainty in the behavior of resource users. Fishers and fishery policies are affected by costly, imperfect enforcement of fisheries law (Sutinen & Andersen, 1985). Therefore, the response of fishers to regulations should be considered when the expectations of implementation, execution and surveillance of a specific management strategy are evaluated (Sutinen *et al.*, 1990). The simplest approach is to assume that the regulations will not be violated and that a free-rider behavior will not occur (Hilborn & Peterman, 1996; see also Chapter 1). However, variations in the dynamic behavior of fishers concerning their allocation of fishing effort, selection of the target species and the fishing gear, and the reliability of catch and effort data reported, could change as a response of changes in management regulations. The dynamic behavior and responses of resource users to regulations should ideally be incorporated into stock assessments in order to mitigate uncertainty levels associated with the forecasted outcomes of management actions (Hilborn & Peterman, 1996; see also Rosenberg & Brault, 1993). When the nature of the regulatory sector is such that its behavior is unpredictable (see below), fishers behavior will be seriously affected and will tend to increase fishing intensity, with the obvious effect on both stock size and profit levels.

6. Uncertainty in future management objectives. Management strategies should be periodically revised and adapted to the dynamic conditions of the stock and resource users, as well as to changes in the intertemporal preferences of the fishing sector. Changes in management objectives resulting from an unpredictable behavior of the regulatory sector constitute an important source of uncertainty (Anderson, 1984). Policy makers will tend to maximize their utility or satisfaction functions, which are subjected to their financial budget and political capital (Niskanen, 1971). In this context, Anderson (1984) introduces the concept of *bioregunomic equilibrium*, which occurs when the biological, economic and regulation components achieve equilibrium simultaneously. Anderson views regulation as endogenous to the fishery system, in which government is seen as the producer or supplier of regulation and the fishers as demanders of regulation. He describes the behavior of marginal and average costs and benefits when introducing this regulation component. According to the model, three basic points exist: open-access equilibrium, bioregunomic equilibrium and the socially optimal level of effort. These points do not necessarily occur at the same fishing effort level. Anderson considers constant prices, and describes the behavior of the regulator trying to select that combination of yield and profit that will maximize his utility, as he must satisfy the demands of several groups (*e.g.*, consumers and producers of fish) involved in the fishery. In this sense, uncertainty in the preference functions of policy makers could be represented by a series of indifference curves of costs and profits, whose shape and position will depend upon the negotiation, political and economic power of each group of the society involved (see Anderson, 1982a, b; 1984).

7. Uncertainty in economic, political and social future conditions. Uncertainty in species price according to market fluctuations, as well as in fixed/variable costs of fishing effort, could influence the dynamic behavior of users. Consequently, the magnitude of catches and related fishing mortality might vary in the short-term, with obvious effects in population abundance. Changes in both local and international political conditions may also constitute a source of uncertainty and could determine different responses of fishers to regulations, especially in cases of political instability and scarcity of employment. This is extremely important in cases of shared resources among developing countries, where the costs of monitoring, control and surveillance depends on international political agreements rather than in enforcement efforts provided by a single country. Moreover, variations in welfare levels of artisanal coastal communities, caused by endogenous (*i.e.*, variations in stock abundance) or exogenous (*e.g.*, changes in species price in the international market) factors, could add uncertainty to the fishery system. These biological, economic or market uncertainties affect expected profits and consequently the short-term dynamic behavior of the fishing fleet. A sudden increase in fishing mortality generally occurs as a result of uncertainty as to future modifications in the regulatory process, because fishers will not be sure of the benefits that will follow from the regulatory measures.

7.3. Management decisions without mathematical probabilities

Three levels of **risk** in the attitude of the manager can be distinguished in decision theory (Pearce & Nash, 1981; Schmid, 1989). (1) A decision-maker who is satisfied to be acting on the basis of expected values, without considering the variance of the different outcomes of decisions, is referred to as *risk neutral*. (2) A *risk averse* decision maker assigns to uncertain prospects as to future costs and benefits of alternative management strategies, certainty equivalencies lower than the expected values. (3) A policy-maker that assigns to future and uncertain economic rents, certainty equivalencies greater than the expected values, is *risk prone*. In practice, a continuous gradient of risk aversion is observed with more than three discrete categories.

Where there are inadequate observations to assign probabilities of occurrence to dissimilar states of nature that have occurred, decision tables could be used to represent different degrees of management caution through the *Maximin, Minimax* and *Maximax* criteria. *Maximin* is a cautious approach that consists in selecting the management decision that involves the maximum Net Present Value *(NPV)* of the observed minimum outcome. It is used when the policy maker is risk averse. When he is less cautious, the *Minimax regret* criterion could be used. This approach selects the management action that minimizes the maximum regret, defined as the difference between the real benefit and the one that could have been obtained if the correct decision had been taken. Finally, an optimist and risk prone policy maker could use the *Maximax* approach, by selecting the management option with the higher *NPV* (see FAO, 1995a; Pérez & Defeo, 1996).

The above decision criteria could be incorporated in the bioeconomic models described in Chapters 2 and 3. Thus, uncertainty in the biological, economic and social processes should be included when developing management advice. For this purpose, several states of nature (*SN*) could be considered for critical parameters (*e.g.*, natural mortality rate, species price, *MSY*, *MEY*), and also for hypotheses about the behavior of many bioeconomic processes (*e.g.* heterogeneity in the spatial distribution of the stock, or strategies for spatial allocation of fishing intensity). This will result in different performances of biological and economic variables if alternative management decisions $D_1, D_{2 \ldots}, D_5$ are taken.

Illustrative example

Consider that the number of observations is insufficient to assign probabilities to SN_1 and SN_2 (*e.g.*, two observed recruitment levels). The risk and uncertainty associated with three alternative management decisions D_1, D_2, D_3 are incorporated, and fishery performance as a function of the *NPV* for these decisions are presented for each state of the nature in a decision table *without mathematical probabilities*. Different degrees of management caution are highlighted through the *Maximin*, *Minimax* and *Maximax* criteria (Tables 7.1 to 7.3).

Table 7.1. The *Maximin* criterion.

Decision	*NPV* of states of nature		Minimum *NPV*
	SN_1	SN_2	
D_1	-30	400	-30
$\boldsymbol{D_2}$	80	150	***80***
D_3	50	300	50

Decision criterion: Select the management strategy with the maximum *NPV* of the minimum outcome: $\boldsymbol{D_2}$

Table 7.2. The *Minimax* regret criterion, and the regret decision table (US$ '000).

Decision	Regret for each decision		Maximum Regret
	SN_1	SN_2	
D_1	80 - (-30) = 110	400 – 400 = 0	110
D_2	80 – 80 = 0	400 – 150 = 250	250
$\boldsymbol{D_3}$	80 – 50 = 30	400 – 300 = 100	***100***

Decision criterion: Select the management action that minimizes the maximum regret: $\boldsymbol{D_3}$

Table 7.3. The *Maximax* criterion.

Decision	*NPV* of states of nature		Maximum *NPV*
	SN_1	SN_2	
$\boldsymbol{D_1}$	-30	400	***400***
D_2	80	150	150
D_3	50	300	300

Decision criterion: Select the management strategy which provides the maximum *NPV*: $\boldsymbol{D_1}$

7.4. Management decisions with mathematical probabilities

Decision theory provides an excellent framework for management advice. The analysis includes stochastic outcomes for a fishery model that considers uncertainty in its parameters and variables, and also in the structure of the model. The outcomes of alternative management actions can thus be evaluated by means of a decision table containing hypotheses about parameter values or model structure and the referred management alternatives (Hilborn & Peterman, 1996).

When considering mathematical probabilities of fishery performance (P_λ) associated with λ possible states of nature *SN* (*e.g.*, recruitment 20% higher or lower than its average), it is possible to estimate the expected value (*EV*) of the *NPV* resulting from different management decisions ($D_1, D_2, \ldots, D_\xi$):

$$EV_\xi = \sum_\lambda P(SN_\lambda) \cdot NPV_{\lambda\xi} \qquad \textbf{(7.1)}$$

The corresponding variance (*VAR*) could be estimated as:

$$VAR_\xi = \sum_\lambda P(SN_\lambda) \cdot (NPV_{\lambda\xi} - EV_\xi)^2 \qquad \textbf{(7.2)}$$

In these cases, the policy maker must do a balance between the expected value and the variances of alternative management decisions (see below).

The example that follows considers again two possible states of nature corresponding to two observed recruitment levels, but now with probabilities of occurrence P_1= .75, P_2= .25. The risk and uncertainty associated with D_1, D_2, D_3 are incorporated, and the *NPV* for these decisions, are presented for each *SN* in Table 7.4.

Table 7.4. *NPV* (US$ '000) of three alternative management strategies (D_1, D_2, D_3) under two states of nature (SN_1,SN_2) with the corresponding probabilities of occurrence P_1 and P_2. *EV*: expected value; *VAR*: variance; *SD*: standard deviation.

Decision	States of nature		*EV*	*VAR*	*SD*
	SN_1 (P_1=.75)	SN_2 (P_2=.25)			
D_1	-30	400	77.5	34668	186
D_2	80	150	97.5	919	39
D_3	50	300	112.5	11719	108

The maximum expected value of *NPV* is generated by D_3. However, *VAR* is greater for D_3 than for D_2, and thus the policy maker must decide between both actions, balancing *EV* and *VAR*.

The Bayesian approach

In the previous section, the *Minimax* principle suggested that we proceed according to a distribution defined over few alternative states. However, there is no reason to expect that nature behave according to this distribution. In some situations, the decision-maker has some information about possible states of nature that allow him to judge *a priori* which state of nature is more likely to be true. Such information can usually be expressed as a probability distribution, considering the state of nature as a random variable. This distribution is referred as a *prior* distribution. *Prior* distributions are often subjective, and depend on the experience or intuition of an individual.

A procedure for utilizing a *prior* to aid in the selection of alternative management actions is the Bayesian Criterion. When prior probabilities can be assigned to different states of nature and management options, the Bayesian approach could be most appropriate for fisheries stock assessment problems (Hilborn & Mangel, 1997 and references therein). The Bayes' Theorem prompts the decision maker to select an action (D_ξ) that minimizes the expected loss ($LOSS\ (D_\xi)$), which is evaluated with respect to a prior distribution ($P(SN_\lambda)$) defined over the possible λ states of nature (SN_λ), where ξ are alternative management options.

$$E\left[LOSS(D_\xi)\right] = \sum_{\lambda} LOSS(NPV_{\lambda\xi} \cdot P(SN_\lambda)) \qquad \textbf{(7.3)}$$

The Bayesian approach could be applied to the above example as follows (Table 7.5):

Table 7.5. The *Bayesian* criterion (US$ '000).

Decision	Loss matrix with *prior* probabilities		Expected Value
	$SN_1 (P_1=.75)$	$SN_2 (P_2=.25)$	
D_1	80 - (-30) = 110	400 - 400 = 0	82.5
D_2	80 - 80 = 0	400 - 150 = 250	62.5
D_3	80 – 50 = 30	400 - 300 = 100	***47.5***

Decision criterion: Select the management strategy which provides the minimum expected losses: D_3

Other decision tables could be built with different performance variables (*e.g.,* biomass, yield, employment, etc.). A detailed analysis of the Bayesian approach as applied in ecology and fisheries stock assessment is beyond the scope of this book. For a complete description, the reader must refer to Hilborn & Mangel (1997) and references therein.

7.5. Estimation of uncertainty in model parameters

Even though highly recommended in the fisheries literature (*e.g.*, Hilborn & Walters, 1992), there are few examples of the estimation of uncertainty (variance) in the management parameters of surplus production models (Kizner, 1990; Polacheck *et al.*, 1993; Punt & Hilborn, 1996). This has substantial importance, because a precautionary approach to management specifically requires a comprehensive treatment of risk and uncertainty in critical management parameters known as reference points (*e.g.*, F_{MSY}, Z_{MSY}, *MSY;* FAO, 1993). In order to use fishery models as explicitly predictive, it is necessary to build confidence intervals that account for the variability around the mean estimates of the parameters. In the case of linear models or those that could be linearised through for example, logarithmic transformations, confidence intervals could be built based on linear classical statistics (Zar, 1984). However, most fishing models are nonlinear, and thus confidence intervals can be calculated by computer intensive methods, such as "jackknife" and "bootstrap" (Efrón, 1979; 1981; 1982).

"Jackknife-bootstrap" estimations for confidence intervals

Jackknife

The "jackknife" consists of sequentially sampling with substitution a pair of data from a base of *n* data pairs corresponding to a series of *n* years of *e.g.,* catch and effort data. Thus, *n* groups of *n-1* data sets are generated, which provide *n* estimates of biological/management parameters. The confidence interval calculated by "jackknife" could be estimated using the classical procedures of linear statistics, assuming that the probabilistic density functions of the parameters are normal ("jackknife normal based" *sensu* Meyer *et al.*, 1986).

Although this constitutes a potentially useful technique for building confidence intervals (Hilborn & Walters, 1992), its application has been questioned. The "jackknife" can be ineffective in providing variance estimates with the usual moderately short fisheries time series, and in such cases do not always provide a clear distribution of the management parameters (Caddy & Defeo, 1996).

Bootstrap

This is based on two different approaches (Efron, 1982; Manly, 1991): random resampling of: (1) the original values in the data set; and (2) the errors derived from the estimations vs observations used to fit a given fishery model (see Punt & Hilborn, 1996).

"Bootstrap" with original data. This technique is based on random resampling with replacement of the original set of *n* (yearly) data pairs corresponding to a particular fishery model (*e.g.*, annual series of catch-effort, total catch-mortality, stock-recruitment). Thus, any of the *n* data pairs corresponding to a given year could be reused multiple times in successive bootstrap estimates.

"Bootstrap" based on errors. In this case, observed data is fitted to a certain fishery model, and the predictions of the dependent variable *Y* generated are then subtracted from the observed ones, obtaining the term of error *e* for each one of the *n* observations. These errors are randomly resampled with replacement and assigned to a certain *Y* predicted value, thus generating a new group of *Y* data. This group of data is used jointly with the independent variable *X* in order to refit the model.

A minimum of 500 "bootstrap" replicates is suggested to estimate confidence bounds (Punt & Hilborn, 1996). The mean and confidence intervals of each parameter could be estimated in two ways: (1) When the probabilistic density functions of the parameters are symmetric and they can be assumed to follow a normal curve, the mean and confidence intervals could be estimated following classical parametric statistics. (2) When parameter distributions are asymmetric, the percentile method is a useful tool for enclosing a given percentage of the bootstrap distribution, in order to provide an empirical confidence interval. In this case, the median is an unbiased and more informative estimate than the mean (Meyer *et al.*, 1986).

Caddy & Defeo (1996) applied version (1) of bootstrap to equilibrium versions of the logistic and exponential versions of the yield-mortality models mentioned in Chapter 2. Confidence limits were obtained directly for the population (M, B_{∞} and r) and management (F_{MSY}, Z_{MSY}, MSY) parameters, from the pool of bootstrap estimates, using the quartile approach. Given the skewed nature of almost all distributions, they determined the median, and calculated the 10th and 90th percentile values that enclosed the central 80% of the bootstrap distribution as the empirical confidence interval. Chapter 2 also shows an additional application of bootstrapping, directed to quantify variability in the parameters of a bioeconomic yield-mortality model (see also Punt & Hilborn, 1996 for a detailed application of bootstrapping to biomass dynamic models).

Due to the asymmetric nature of almost all the parameters distribution functions generated by fishery models, resampling the residuals together with the application of the percentile theory seems to be a useful method. It preserves the "design" of the study, by using the original values of the independent variable, and also diminishes the probability of obtaining negative values (Pérez & Defeo, 1996).

Risk analysis and "bootstrap"

Caddy & Defeo (1996) elaborated a simple approach to formulation of risk-averse management strategies, using the percentiles of a cumulative distribution of *MSY* estimates from bootstrapping against Z, which it is suggested would allow fishery management advice to be generated based on annual mortality and yield vectors alone. The bootstrap distribution for Z_{MSY} obtained by equations developed in Chapter 2 suggests a simple way of using this fitting procedure in a management context, where Z values (from size frequency analysis) could be used as a management control variable, and where the risk of making a wrong management decision is a real one. A cumulative distribution of values of *MSY* with Z from bootstrapping provided the basis for evaluating a proposed management target. This might be either framed in terms of F (M known), or simply using the Z value expected for a given management action as the control variable which provide feedback on the impact of fishing. The probability that a given value Z_{now} will exceed Z_{MSY} in the current year of fishing could be determined by this procedure. This simple risk analysis could be carried out by bootstrapping the results of the different models provided in Chapter 2.

The "bootstrap" procedure provides further advantages for selecting management options in a probabilistic context. For example, taking into account that the values of M, r and management parameters from a single bootstrap fit are all cross-correlated, a manager seeking advice about what to do on the basis of a fit of the models described here, should primarily consider what would be the most precautionary parameter set to adopt, *i.e.*, which would be the one least likely to lead to overexploitation.

Other procedures related to the estimation of risk and uncertainty for scientific advice in fisheries are beyond the scope of this document. The reader is referred to FAO (1996) and Francis & Shotton (1997) among other relevant scientific papers on the subject.

References

Acheson, J. & R. Reidman. 1982. Biological and economic effects of increasing the minimum legal size of American lobster in Maine. *Trans. Amer. Fish. Soc.* 111: 1-12.

Ackoff, R.L. 1962. *Scientific method: Optimizing Applied Research Decisions*. J. Wiley & Sons, New York.

Agnello, R.J. & L.G. Anderson. 1983. Production responses for multi-species fisheries. *Can. J. Fish. Aquat. Sci.* 38: 1393-1404.

Agnello, R.J. & L.P. Donnelley. 1976. Externalities and property rights in the fisheries. *Land Econ.* 52: 518-529.

Akenhead, S.A., J. Carscadden, H. Learn, G.R. Lilly & R. Wells. 1982. Cod-capelin interactions off Northeast Newfoundland and Labrador. In: Mercer, M.D. (ed.), *Multispecies Approaches to Fisheries Management Advice. Can. Spec. Publ. Fish. Aquat. Sci.* 59: 141-148.

Alverson, D.L., M.H. Freeberg, J.G. Pope & S.A. Murawski. 1994. A global assessment of fisheries bycatch and discards. *FAO Fish. Tech. Pap.* (339): 233 pp.

Anderson, L.G. 1975a. Analysis of open-access commercial exploitation and maximum economic yield in biological and technologically interdependent fisheries. *J. Fish. Res. Bd. Can.* 32: 1825-1842.

Anderson, L.G. 1975b. Optimum economic yield of an internationally utilized common property resource. *Fish. Bull.* 73: 51-66.

Anderson, L.G. 1977. *The Economics of Fisheries Management*. The John Hopkins University Press, New York.

Anderson, L.G. 1980. A comparison of limited entry fisheries management schemes. In: ACMRR *Working Party on the Scientific Basis of Determining Management Measures*, FAO Fish. Rep. 236: 47-74.

Anderson, L.G. 1981. *Economic Analysis for Fisheries Management Plans*. Ann Arbor Science Publishers, Michigan.

Anderson, L.G 1982a. Optimal utilization of fisheries with increasing costs of effort. *Can. J. Fish. Aquat. Sci.* 39: 211-214.

Anderson, L.G. 1982b. An economic analysis of joint recreational and commercial fisheries. In: Grover, J.H. (ed.), *Allocation of Fishery Resources*. Proceedings of the Technical Consultation, Vichy, France, 1980. FAO/AFS: 16-26.

Anderson, L.G. 1984. Uncertainty in the fisheries management process. *Mar. Res. Econ.* 1: 77-87.

Anderson, L.G. 1986. *The Economics of Fisheries Management*. Revised and enlarged edition. The John Hopkins University Press, Baltimore.

Anderson, L.G. 1994. Fundamental issues in the design of ITQ programs. In: Antona, M., J. Catanzano & J. Sutinen (ed.), *Proceedings of the sixth conference of the International Institute of Fisheries Economics and Trade*. Paris, Francia. Tome II: 787-801.

Anderson, L.G. 1995. Privatizing open access fisheries: individual transferable quotas. In: Bromley, D. W. (ed.), *Handbook of Environmental Economics*. Blackwell Publishers, Cambridge, Mass.: 453-474.

Anonymous, 1995. *Solving Bycatch: Considerations for Today and Tomorrow.* Alaska Sea Grant College Program Report No. 96-03, University of Alaska Fairbanks.

Arrow, K.J. 1976. *Social Choice and Individual Values*. 2nd edition. J. Wiley & Sons, New York.

Baranov, F.I. 1918. On the question of the biological basis of fisheries. *Nauchn. Issled. Ikhtiologicheskii Inst. Izv.* 1: 81-128.

Beddington, J.R. 1984. The response of multispecies systems to perturbations. In: May, R.M. (ed.), *Exploitation of Marine Communities.* Dahlem Konferenzen 1984. Springer-Verlag, Berlin: 209-225.

Beddington, J.R. & R.B. Rettig. 1984. Criterios para la ordenación del esfuerzo de pesca. *FAO Doc. Tec. Pesca* (243): 44 pp.

Begon, M., J.L. Harper & C.R. Townsend. 1990. *Ecology. Individuals, Populations and Communities.* Blackwell Scientific Publications, Boston.

Berkes, F. (Ed.). 1989. *Common Property Resources: Ecology and Community-Based Sustainable Development.* Belhaven Press, London.

Bertalanffy, L., von. 1938. A quantitative theory of organic growth. *Hum. Biol.* 10: 191-213.

Beverton, R.J.H. & S.J. Holt. 1954. Notes on the use of theoretical models in the study of the dynamics of exploited fish populations. U.S. Fish. Lab., Beaufort, N.C., Misc. Contrib 2: 159 pp.

Beverton, R.J.H. & S.J. Holt. 1957. *On the Dynamics of Exploited Fish Populations. Fish. Invest. London. Ser.* II. 19: 1-533.

Bockstael, N. & J. Opaluch. 1983. Discrete modeling of supply response under uncertainty: the case of the fishery. *J. Environ. Econ. Manag.* 10: 125-136.

Bosman, A.L., P.A. Hockey & W.R. Siegfried. 1987. The influence of coastal upwelling on the functional structure of rocky intertidal communities. *Oecologia.* (Berlin) 72: 226-232.

Botsford, L.W. 1986. Effects of environmental forcing on age-structured populations: northern California Dungeness crab (*Cancer magister*) as an example. *Can. J. Fish. Aquat. Sci.* 43: 2245-2352.

Botsford, L., J.C. Castilla & C.H. Peterson. 1997. The management of fisheries and marine ecosystems. Science 277: 509-515.

Box, J.M. 1965. A new method of constrained optimization and a comparison with other methods. *Computer J.* 8: 42-52.

Bromley, W.D. 1991. Testing for common versus private property: comment. *J. Environ. Econ. Manag.* 21: 92-96.

Bustamante, R. & J.C. Castilla. 1987. La pesquería de mariscos en Chile: un análisis de 26 años de desembarques (1960-1985). *Biol. Pesq.* (Chile) 16: 79-97.

Bustamante, R. & J.C. Castilla. 1990. Impact of human explotation on populations of the intertidal southern bull-kelp *Durvillaea antarctica* (Phaeophyta, Durvilleales) in Central Chile. *Biol. Conserv.* 52: 205-220.

Caddy, J.F. 1975. Spatial model for an exploited shellfish population, and its application to the Georges Bank scallop fishery. *J. Fish. Res. Bd. Can.* 32: 1305-1328.

Caddy, J.F. 1979. Some considerations underlying definitions of catchability and fishing effort in shellfish fisheries, and their relevance for stock assessment purposes. *Fish. Mar. Serv., Manuscr. Rep.* 1489: 1-18.

Caddy, J.F. 1986. Stock assessment in data-limited situations - the experience in tropical fisheries and its possible relevance to evaluation of invertebrate resources. In: Jamieson, G.S. & N. Bourne (ed.), *North Pacific Workshop on Stock Assessment and Management of Invertebrates. Can. Spec. Publ. Fish. Aquat. Sci.* 92: 379-392.

Caddy, J.F. 1989a. A perspective on the population dynamics and assessment of scallop fisheries, with special reference to the sea scallop *Placopecten magellanicus* Gmelin. In: Caddy, J.F. (ed.), *Marine Invertebrate Fisheries: Their Assessment and Management.* J. Wiley & Sons, New York: 559-590.

Caddy, J.F. 1989b. Recent developments in research and management for wild stocks of bivalves and gastropods. In: Caddy, J.F. (ed.), *Marine Invertebrate Fisheries: Their Assessment and Management.* J. Wiley & Sons, New York: 665-700.

Caddy, J.F. 1996. Regime shifts and paradigm changes: is there still a place for equilibrium thinking? *Fish. Res.* 25: 219-230.

Caddy, J.F. & J. Csirke. 1983. Approximation to sustainable yield for exploited and unexploited stocks. *Oceanogr. Trop.* 18(1): 3-15.

Caddy, J.F. & O. Defeo. 1996. Fitting the exponential and logistic surplus yield models with mortality data: some explorations and new perspectives. *Fish. Res.* 25: 39-62.

Caddy, J.F. & J.A. Gulland. 1983. Historical patterns of fish stocks. *Mar. Pol.* 7: 267-278.

Caddy, J.F. & R. Mahon. 1995. Reference points for fisheries management. *FAO Fish. Tech. Pap.* (347): 83 pp.

Caddy, J.F. & G.D. Sharp. 1986. An ecological framework for marine fishery investigations. *FAO Fish. Tech. Pap.* (283): 152 pp.

Castilla, J.C. 1994. The chilean small-scale benthic shellfisheries and the institutionalization of new management practices. *Ecol. Int. Bull.* 21: 47-63.

Castilla, J.C. & R. Durán. 1985. Human exclusion from the rocky intertidal zone of Central Chile: the effects on *C. concholepas* (Mollusca: Gastropoda: Muricidae). *Oikos* 45: 391-399.

Castilla, J.C., P. Manríquez, J. Alvarado, A. Rosson, C. Pino, C. Espoz, R. Soto, D. Oliva & O. Defeo. 1998. Artisanal "caletas" as units of production and co-managers of benthic invertebrates in Chile. In: Jamieson, J.G. & A. Campbell (eds.), *Proceedings of the North Pacific Symposium on Invertebrate Stock Assessment and Management. Can. Spec. Publ. Fish. Aquat. Sci.* 125: 407-413.

Charles, A.T. 1989. Bio-socio-economic fishery models: labour dynamics and multi-objective management. *Can. J. Fish. Aquat. Sci.* 46: 1313-1322.

Charles, A.T. 1995. Bio-socio-economic modelling and management options in invertebrate fisheries. In: Jamieson, J.G. & A. Campbell (eds.), *Proceedings of the North Pacific Symposium on Invertebrate Stock Assessment and Management.* Abstract, p. 27.

Charles, A.T. & A. Herrera. 1994. Development and diversification: sustainability strategies for a Costa Rica Fishing Cooperative. In: Antona, M., J. Catanzano & J. Sutinen (ed.), *Proceedings of the sixth conference of the International Institute of Fisheries Economics and Trade.* Paris, Francia, Tome II: 1315-1324.

Chenney, W. & D. Kincaid. 1985. *Numerical Mathematics and Computing.* Brooks Cole Publishing Company, Monterey, California.

Clark, C.W. 1973. Profit maximization and the extinction of animal species. *J. Polit. Econ.* 81: 950-961.

Clark, C.W. 1976. *Mathematical Bioeconomics: The Optimal Management of Renewable Resources.* J. Wiley & Sons, New York.

Clark, C.W. 1985. *Bioeconomic Modelling of Fisheries Management.* J. Wiley & Sons, New York.

Cobb, J.S. & J.F. Caddy. 1989. The population biology of decapods. In: Caddy, J.F. (ed.), *Marine Invertebrate Fisheries: Their Assessment and Management.* J. Wiley & Sons, New York: 327-374.

Cohen, Y. 1987. A review of harvest theory and applications of optimal control theory in fisheries management. *Can. J. Fish. Aquat. Sci.* 44(Suppl. 2): 75-83.

Conan, G.Y. 1984. Do assumptions commonly used for modelling populations of finfish apply to shellfish species? ICES, *Shellfish Committee, C.M.* 1984/K: 49: 21 pp.

Csirke, J. & J.F. Caddy. 1983. Production modelling using mortality estimates. *Can. J. Fish. Aquat. Sci.* 40: 43-51.

De Anda, J.A., J.C. Seijo & S. Martínez. 1994. Reclutamiento y variabilidad ambiental en la pesquería de sardina Monterrey (*Sardinops sagax*) del Golfo de California, México. *Invest. Pesq.* (Chile) 38: 23-36.

Defeo, O. 1989. Development and management of artisanal fishery for yellow clam *Mesodesma mactroides* in Uruguay. *Fishbyte* 7: 21-25.

Defeo, O. 1993a. The effect of spatial scales in population dynamics and modelling of sedentary fisheries: the yellow clam *Mesodesma mactroides* of an Uruguayan exposed sandy beach. Ph.D. Thesis, *CINVESTAV-IPN Unidad Mérida*, Yucatán, México. 308 pp.

Defeo, O. 1993b. Repopulation of coastal invertebrates through the management on natural areas: a successful example. *Out of the Shell* 3: 11-13.

Defeo, O. 1996. Experimental management of an exploited sandy beach bivalve population. *Rev. Chil. Hist. Nat.* 69: 605-614.

Defeo, O. 1998. Testing hypotheses on recruitment, growth and mortality in exploited bivalves: an experimental perspective. In: Jamieson, J.G. & A. Campbell (ed.), *Proceedings of the North Pacific Symposium on Invertebrate Stock Assessment and Management. Can. Spec. Publ. Fish. Aquat. Sci.* 125: 257-264.

Defeo O. & A. de Alava. 1995. Effects of human activities on long-term trends in sandy beach populations: the wedge clam *Donax hanleyanus* in Uruguay. *Mar. Ecol. Prog. Ser.* 123: 73-82.

Defeo O. & J.C. Seijo. (in press). Yield-mortality models: a precautionary bioeconomic approach. *Fish. Res.*

Defeo, O., A. de Alava, V. Valdivieso & J.C. Castilla. 1993. Historical landings and management options for the genus *Mesodesma* in coasts of South America. *Biol. Pesq.* (Chile) 22: 41-54.

Defeo, O., J.C. Seijo, J. Euan & M. Liceaga. 1991. Dinámica espacial del esfuerzo pesquero de una pesquería artesanal de la costa Atlántica Uruguaya. *Invest. Pesq.* (Chile). 36: 17-25.

Díaz de León, A.J. & J.C. Seijo. 1992. A multi-criteria non-linear optimization model for the control and management of a tropical fishery. *Mar. Res. Econ.* 7: 23-40.

Durán, L.R. & J.C. Castilla. 1989. Variation and persistence of the middle rocky intertidal community of Central Chile, with and without human harvesting. *Mar. Biol.* 103: 555-562.

Durán, R., J.C. Castilla & D. Oliva. 1987. Intensity of human predation on rocky shores at Las Cruces, Central Chile. *Environ. Conserv.* 14: 143-149.

Eales, J. & J.W. Wilen. 1986. An examination of fishing location choice in the pink shrimp fishery. *Mar. Res. Econ.* 2: 331-351.

Eckert, R. 1979. *The Enclosure of Ocean Resources.* Hoover Institution Press, Stanford California.

Efron, B. 1979. Bootstrap methods: another look at the jackknife. *Ann. Stat.* 7: 1-26.

Efron, B. 1981. Non parametric estimates of standard error: the jackknife, the bootstrap and other methods. *Biometrika* 68: 589-599.

Efron, B. 1982. *The Jackknife, the Bootstrap and other Resampling Plans.* Society for Industrial and Applied Mathematics, Philadelphia, Pennsylvania.

Elliot, J.M. 1977. *Some Methods for the Statistical Analysis of Samples of Benthic Invertebrates* (2nd. ed.). Freshwater Biol. Assoc. Sci. Publ. 25.

Emerson, W. & J. Anderson. 1989. A spatial allocation model for the New England fisheries. *Mar. Res. Econ.* 6: 123-144.

Estes, J.A. & J.F. Palmisano. 1974. Sea otters: their role in structuring nearshore communities. *Science* 185: 1058-1060.

FAO. 1978. Fishery commodity situation and outlook. *FAO: Com. Fish.* 12th Session, COFI/78/inf. 5: 1-15.

FAO. 1993. Reference Points for fishery management: their potential application to straddling and highly migratory resources. *FAO Fish. Circ.* (864): 52 pp.

FAO. 1994. Review of the state of world marine fishery resources. *FAO Fish. Tech. Pap.* (335): 136 pp.

FAO. 1995a. Precautionary approach to fisheries. Part 1: Guidelines on the precautionary approach to capture fisheries and species introductions. *FAO Fish. Tech. Pap.* (350/1): 52 pp.

FAO. 1995b. World fisheries: problems and prospects. *FAO Committee of Fisheries Document.* COFI/95/3Inf. 3: 13 pp.

FAO. 1996. Precautionary approach to fisheries. Part 2: Scientific papers. *FAO Fish. Tech. Pap.* (350/2): 210 pp.

Farzin, Y.H. 1984. The effect of the discount rate on depletion of exhaustible resources. *J. Polit. Econ.* 92: 841-851.

Fogarty, M.J. 1989. Forecasting yield and abundance of exploited invertebrates. In: Caddy, J.F. (ed.), *Marine Invertebrate Fisheries: Their Assessment and Management*. J. Wiley & Sons, New York: 701-724.

Fox, W.W. 1970. An exponential surplus yield model for optimizing exploited fish populations. *Trans. Am. Fish. Soc.* 99: 80-88.

Francis, R.I.C.C. & R. Shotton. 1997. "Risk" in fisheries management: a review. *Can. J. Fish. Aquat. Sci.* 54: 1699-1715.

Garcia, S.M. 1992. Ocean fisheries management: the FAO programme. In: Fabbri, P. (ed.), *Ocean Management and Global Change*. Elsevier Applied Science, London: 381-418.

Garcia, S.M. 1996. The precautionary approach to fisheries and its implications for fishery research, technology and management: an updated review. In: *Precautionary Approach to Fisheries. Part 2: Scientific papers. FAO Fish. Tech. Pap.* (350/2): 1-75.

Garcia, S.M. & A. Demetropoulos. 1986. Management of Cyprus fisheries. *FAO Fish. Tech. Pap.* (250): 40 pp.

Garcia, S.M. & C. Newton. 1994. Responsible fisheries: an overview of FAO policy developments (1945-1994). *Mar. Poll. Bull.* 29: 528-536.

Garcia, S.M. & C. Newton. 1997. Curent situation, trends, and prospects in world capture fisheries. In: Pikitch, E.K., D.D. Huppert & M.P. Sissenwine (ed.), *Global Trends in Fisheries Management.* American Fisheries Society Symposium, 20, Bethesda, Maryland: 3-27.

Garrod, D.J. & J.G. Shepherd. 1981. On the relationship between fishing capacity and resource allocations. In: Haley, K.B. (ed.), *Prcceedings of a NATO Symposium on Applied Operations Research in Fishing.* Plenum Press, New York: 321-336.

Gause, G.F. & A.A. Witt. 1935. Behavior of mixed populations and the problem of natural selection. *Am. Nat.* 69: 596-609.

Geen, G. & M. Nayar. 1988. Individual transferable quotas in the Southern bluefin tuna fishery: an economic appraisal. *Mar. Res. Econ.* 5: 365-387.

Gillis, D.M., R.M. Peterman & A.V. Tyler. 1993. Movement dynamics in a fishery: application of the ideal free distribution to spatial allocation of effort. Can. *J. Fish. Aquat. Sci.* 50: 323-333.

Gordon, H.S. 1953. An economic approach to the optimum utilization of fishery resources. *J. Fish. Res. Bd. Can.* 10: 442-447.

Gordon, H.S. 1954. The economics of a common property resource: the fishery. *J. Polit. Econ.* 62: 124-142.

Gottfried, B.S. 1984. *Elements of Stochastic Process Simulation.* Prentice-Hall, Inc., Englewood Cliffs.

Graham, M. 1935. Modern theory of exploiting a fishery and application to North Sea trawling. *J. Cons. Int. Explor. Mer.* 10: 264-274.

Graybeal, W.J. & W.W. Pooch. 1980. *Simulation Principles and Methods*. Winthrop Publishers, Inc. Cambridge, Mass.

Gulland, J.A. 1983. *Fish Stock Assessment: A Manual of Basic Methods*. J. Wiley & Sons, New York.

Gulland, J.A. & S.M. Garcia. 1984. Observed patterns in multispecies fisheries, In: May, R.M. (ed.), *Exploitation of Marine Communities*. Dahlem Konferenzen 1984. Springer-Verlag, Berlln: 155-190.

Hall, M. A. 1983. A spatial approach to the population dynamics of the manila clam (*Tapes philippinarum*). Ph.D. Dissertation, *University of Washington*: 244 pp.

Hall, M. A. 1996. On bycatches. *Rev. Fish Biol. Fish.* 6: 319-352.

Hall, M. A. 1998. An ecological view of the tuna-dolphin problem: impacts and trade-offs. *Rev. Fish Biol. Fish.* 8: 1-34.

Hancock, D.A. 1973. The relationship between stock and recruitment in exploited invertebrates. *Rapp. P.- V. Reun. Cons. Int. Explor. Mer.* 164: 113-131.

Hancock, D.A. 1979. Population dynamics and management of shellfish stocks. In: Thomas, H.J. (ed.), *Population Assessments of Shellfish Stocks. Rapp. P.-V. Réun. Cons. Int. Explor. Mer.* 175: 8-19.

Hannesson, R. 1978. *Economics of Fisheries: An Introduction*. Columbia University Press, New York.

Hannesson, R. 1986. The effect of the discount rate on the optimal exploitation of renewable resources. *Mar. Res. Econ.* 3: 319-329.

Hannesson, R. 1987. Optimal catch capacity and fishing effort in deterministic and stochastic fishery models. *Fish. Res.* 5: 1-21.

Hannesson, R. 1993. *Bioeconomic Analysis of Fisheries*. Fishing News Books, Blackwell, Oxford.

Hilborn, R. & M. Ledbetter. 1979. Analysis of the British Columbia salmon purse seine fleet: dynamics of movement. *J. Fish. Res. Bd. Can.* 36: 384-391.

Hilborn, R. & M. Mangel. 1997. *The Ecological Detective*. Monographs in Population Biology 28, Princeton University Press, Princeton.

Hilborn, R. & R.M. Peterman. 1996. The development of scientific advice with incomplete information in the context of the precautionary approach. In: *Precautionary Approach to Fisheries. Part 2: Scientific papers. FAO Fish. Tech. Pap.* (350/2): 77-101.

Hilborn, R. & C.J. Walters. 1987. A general model for simulation of stock and fleet dynamics in spatially heterogeneous fisheries. *Can. J. Fish. Aquat. Sci.* 44: 1366-1369.

Hilborn, R. & C.J. Walters. 1992. *Quantitative Fisheries Stock Assessment. Choice, Dynamics and Uncertainty*. Chapman & Hall, New York.

Hockey, P.A.R. & A.L. Bosman. 1986. Man as an intertidal predator in Transkei: disturbance, community convergence, and management of a natural food resource. *Oikos* 46: 3-14.

Hoenig, J.M. & N.A. Hoenig. 1986. Fitting stock production models subject to a constraint. U. Rhode Island Dept. Stats. *Tech. Rep.* TR-186: 10 pp.

Hoppensteadt, F.C. & I. Sohn. 1981. A multiple species fishery model: an input-output approach. In: Haley, K.B. (ed.), *Applied Operations Research in Fishing*. NATO Conference Series, Plenum Press, London: 115-124.

Huppert, D. 1979. Implications of multipurpose fleets and mixed stocks for control policies. *J. Fish. Res. Bd. Can.* 36 (7): 845-854.

Issard, W. & P. Liossatos. 1979. *Spatial Dynamics and Optimal Space-Time Development*. North-Holland Publishing Company, New York.

Jamieson, G.S., & J.F. Caddy. 1986. Research advice and its application to management of invertebrate resources: an overview. In: Jamieson, G.S. & N. Bourne (ed.), *North Pacific Workshop on Stock Assessment and Management of Invertebrates. Can. Spec. Publ. Fish. Aquat. Sci.* 92: 416-424.

Kennedy, J.O.S. & J.W. Watkins. 1986. Time-dependent quotas for the southern bluefin tuna fishery. *Mar. Res. Econ.* 2: 293-313.

Kizner, Z.I. 1990. Bootstrap estimation of the confidence intervals of stock and TAC assessments with the use of dynamic surplus production models. *NAFO SCR Doc.* 90/108: 6 pp.

Lapointe, M.F., R.M. Peterman & A. MacCall. 1989. Trends in fishing mortality rate along with errors in natural mortality rate can cause spurious time trends in fish stock abundances estimated by Virtual Population Analysis (VPA). *Can. J. Fish. Aquat. Sci.* 46: 2129-2139.

Lawson, R.M. 1984. *Economics of Fisheries Management*. Praeger Publishers, New York.

Leslie, P.H. & J.C. Gower. 1960. Properties of a stochastic model for the predator-prey type of interaction between two species. *Biometrika* 47: 219-301.

Lewis, T.R. 1982. *Stochastic Modeling of Ocean Fisheries Resource Management*. University of Washington Press, Seattle.

Lotka, A.J. 1932. The growth of mixed populations: two species competing for a common food supply. *J. Wash. Acad. Sci.* 22: 461-469.

Lubchenco, J., G.W. Allison, S.A. Navarrete, B.A. Menge, J.C. Castilla, O. Defeo, C. Folke, O. Kussakin, T. Norton & A.M. Wood. 1995. 6.1.9. Coastal systems. In: United Nations Environment Programme. *Global Biodiversity Assessment*. Section 6: Biodiversity and ecosystem functioning: ecosystem analyses. Cambridge University Press, Cambridge, U.K.: 370-381.

Ludwig, D., R. Hilborn & C. Walters. 1993. Uncertainty, resource exploitation, and conservation: lessons from history. *Science* 260: 17, 36.

MacCall, A.D. 1976. Density-dependence of catchability coefficient in the California Pacific sardine, *Sardinops sagax caerula*, purse seine fishery. California *Coop. Ocean. Fish. Inv. Rep.* 18: 136-148.

Maiolo, R.M. & Orbach, K.M. 1982. *Modernization and Marine Fisheries Policy*. Ann Arbor Science Publishers, Michigan.

Manetsch, T.J. 1976. Time varying distributed delays and their use in aggregate models of large systems. *IEEE Transactions on Systems, Man and Cybernetics*. SMC-6 N°8: 547-553.

Manetsch, T.J. 1985. Planning to meet economic and nutritional goals in developing countries. An application of multi-criteria optimization. Unpublished manuscript, Michigan State University, East Lansing, Michigan.

Manetsch, T.J. 1986. *M-OPTSIM. A Microcomputer Based Program for System Simulation and Optimization*. Michigan State University, East Lansing, Michigan.

Manetsch, T.J. & G.L. Park. 1982. *System Analysis and Simulation with Applications to Economic and Social Systems*. Fourth edition, Michigan State University, Michigan.

Mangel, M. & C.W. Clark. 1983. Uncertainty, search and information in fisheries. *J. Cons. Perm. Int. Explor. Mer.* 48: 93-103.

Manly, B.J. 1991. *Randomization and Monte Carlo Methods in Biology*. Chapman & Hall, London.

Mapstone, B. D., R. A. Campbell, & A. D. M. Smith. 1996. Design of experimental investigations of the effects of line and spear fishing on the Great Barrier Reef. *CRC Reef Research Technical Report* Number 7, C.R.C. Reef Research Centre, James Cook University, Townsville, Queensland, Australia.

May, R.M. (ed.). 1984. *Exploitation of Marine Communities*. Report of the Dahlem Workshop on Exploitation of Marine Communities. Dahlem Konferenzen 1984. Springer-Verlag, Berlin.

May, R.M., J.R. Beddington, C.W. Clark, S.J. Holt & R.M. Laws. 1979. Management of multispecies fisheries. *Science* 205: 267-277.

Mendelssohn, R. 1979. Determining the best trade-off between expected economic return and the risk of undesirable events when managing a randomly varying population. *J. Fish. Res. Bd. Can.* 36: 939-947.

Mercer, M.C. 1982. Multispecies approaches to fisheries management advice. *Can. Spec. Publ. Fish. Aquat. Sci.* 59.

Mesterton-Gibbons, M. 1996. A technique for finding optimal two-species harvesting policies. *Ecol. Model.* 92: 235-244.

Meyer, J.S., C.G. Ingersoll, L.L. McDonald & M.S. Boyce. 1986. Estimating uncertainty in population growth rates: jackknife vs. bootstrap techniques. *Ecology* 67: 1156-1166.

Mitchell, C.L. 1982. Bioeconomics of multispecies exploitation in fisheries: management implications. In: Mercer, M.C. (ed.), *Multispecies Approaches to Fisheries Management Advice. Can. Spec. Publ. Fish. Aquat. Sci.* 59: 157-162.

Moreno, C.A., J.P. Sutherland & H.F. Jara. 1984. Man as a predator in the intertidal zone of southern Chile. *Oikos* 42: 155-160.

Moreno, C.A., K.M. Lunecke & M.I. Lepez. 1986. The response of an intertidal *Concholepas concholepas* population to the protection from man in southern Chile and the effects on benthic sessile assemblages. *Oikos* 46: 359-364.

Morgan G.R. 1997. Individual quota management in fisheries. *FAO Fish. Tech. Pap.* (371): 41 pp.

Niskanen, W.A. 1971. *Bureaucracy and Representative Government*. Aldine-Atherton, Chicago.

Onal, H., B.A. McCarl, W.L. Griffin, G. Matlock, G. & J. Clark. 1991. A bioeconomic analysis of the Texas shrimp fishery and its optimal management. *Am. J. Agr. Econ.* (Nov.): 1161-1170.

Orensanz, J.M. 1986. Size, environment, and density: regulation of a scallop stock and its management implications. In: Jamieson, G.S. & N. Bourne (ed.), *North Pacific Workshop on Stock Assessment and Management of Invertebrates. Can. Spec. Publ. Fish. Aquat. Sci.* 92: 195-227.

Orensanz, J. & G.S. Jamieson 1998. The assessment and management of spatially structured stocks: an overview of the North Pacific Symposium on Invertebrate Stock Assessment and Management. In: Jamieson, J.G. & A. Campbell (ed.), *Proceedings of the North Pacific Symposium on Invertebrate Stock Assessment and Management. Can. Spec. Publ. Fish. Aquat. Sci.* 125: 441-459.

Orensanz, J.M., A.M. Parma & O.O. Iribarne. 1991. Population dynamics and management of natural stocks. In: Shumway, S.E. (ed.), *Scallops: Biology, Ecology and Aquaculture*. Development in Aquaculture and Fisheries Science 21: 625-713.

Ostrom, E. 1990. *Governing to Commons: The Evolution of Institutions for Collective Action*. Cambridge University Press, Cambridge.

Osyczka, A. 1984. *A Multicriterion Optimization in Engineering*. Halsted Press, New York.

Paine, R.T. 1966. Food web complexity and species diversity. *Amer. Nat.* 100: 65-75.

Paine, R.T. 1980. Food webs: linkage, interaction strength and community infrastructure. *J. Anim. Ecol.* 49: 667-685.

Paine, R.T. 1984. Ecological determinism in the competition for space. *Ecology* 65: 1339-1348.

Panayotou, T. 1983. Conceptos de ordenación para las pesquerías en pequeña escala. *FAO, Doc. Tec. Pesca* (228): 60 pp.

Pauly, D. 1982. Studying single-species dynamics in a tropical multispecies context. In: D. Pauly & G.I. Murphy (ed.), *Theory and Management of Tropical Fisheries.* ICLARM Conf. Proc. 9: 33-70.

Pauly, D. & G.I. Murphy. (ed.) 1982. *Theory and Management of Tropical Fisheries.* ICLARM Conf. Proc. 9.

Payne, J.A. 1982. *Introduction to Simulation. Programming Techniques and Methods of Analysis.* McGraw-Hill, New York.

Pearce, D.W. & C.A. Nash. 1981. *Social Appraisal of Projects: A Text in Cost-Benefit Analysis.* Macmillan, London.

Pearse, P.H. 1980. Regulation of fishing effort. *FAO. Fish. Tech. Pap.* (197): 82 pp.

Pella, J.J. & P.K. Tomlinson. 1969. A generalized stock production model. *Bull. Inter-Amer. Trop. Tuna Comm.* 13: 421-496.

Pérez, E. & O. Defeo. 1996. Estimación de riesgo e incertidumbre en modelos de producción captura-mortalidad. *Biol. Pesq.* (Chile) 25: 3-15.

Pinkerton, E. (ed.). 1989. *Cooperative Management of Local Fisheries: New Directions for Improved Management and Community Development.* University of British Columbia Press, Vancouver B. C.

Polacheck, T., R. Hilborn & A.E. Punt. 1993. Fitting surplus production models: comparing methods and measuring uncertainty. *Can. J. Fish. Aquat. Sci.* 50: 2597-2607.

Power, M. 1993. The predictive validation of ecological and environmental models. *Ecol. Modelling* 68: 33-50.

Punt, A.E. & R. Hilborn. 1996. Biomass dynamic models. User's manual. *FAO Comp. Inf. Ser. Fish.* (10): 62 pp.

Randall, A. 1981. *Resource Economics: An Economic Approach to Natural Resource and Environmental Policy.* Grid Publishing Inc., Columbus, Ohio.

Ricker, W.E. 1975. Computation and interpretation of biological statistics of fish populations. *Bull. Fish. Res. Bd. Can.* 191: 382 pp.

Rosenberg, A.A. & S. Brault. 1993. Choosing a management strategy for stock rebuilding when control is uncertain. In: Smith, S.J., J.J. Hunt & D. Rivard (ed.), *Risk Evaluation and Biological Reference Points for Fisheries Management.* Can. Spec. Publ. Fish. Aquat. Sci. 120: 243-249.

Rykiel Jr, E.J. 1996. Testing ecological models : the meaning of validation. *Ecol. Modelling* 90: 229-244.

Saila, S.B. & K. Erzini. 1987. Empirical approach to multispecies stock assessment. *Trans. Am. Fish. Soc.* 116: 601-611.

Sainsbury, K. J. 1987. Assessment and management of the demersal fishery on the continental shelf of northwestern Australia, In: Polovina, J. & S. Ralston (ed.), *Tropical Snappers and Groupers: Biology and Fisheries Management.* Westview Press, Boulder, Colorado: 465-503.

Sainsbury, K.J. 1988. The ecological basis of multispecies fisheries and management of a demersal fishery in Tropical Australia, In: Gulland, J. (ed.), *Fish Population Dynamics.* J. Wiley & Sons, New York: 349-382.

Schaefer, M.B. 1954. Some aspects of the dynamics of populations important to the management of commercial marine fisheries. *Bull. Inter-Amer. Trop. Tunna Comm.* 1: 27-56.

Schelling, T.C. 1978. *Micromotives and Macrobehavior.* W.W. Norton & Company, New York.

Schmid, A.A. 1978. *Property, Power and Public Choice.* Praeger, New York.

Schmid, A.A. 1987. *Property, Power and Public Choice.* 2ed. Praeger, New York.

Schmid, A.A. 1989. *Benefit-Cost Analysis: A Political Economy Approach.* Westview Press. Boulder.

Schnute, J.T. & R. Hilborn. 1993. Analysis of contradictory data sources in fish stock assessment. *Can. J. Fish. Aquat. Sci.* 50: 1916-1923.

Seijo, J.C. 1986. Comprehensive simulation model of a tropical demersal fishery: red grouper (*Epinephelus morio*) of the Yucatan Continental Shelf. Ph.D. Dissertation, *Michigan State University*: 210 pp.

Seijo, J.C. 1987. Modelación de pesquerías tropicales. *XXV Aniv. Inst. Nal. Pesca* (1): 85-90.

Seijo, J.C. 1989. The systems simulation approach to tropical fisheries management, In: Chávez, E.A. (ed.), *Memorias del Seminario México-Australia sobre Ciencias Marinas*: 279-288.

Seijo, J.C. 1993. Individual transferable grounds in a community managed artisanal fishery. *Mar. Res. Econ.* 8: 78-81.

Seijo, J.C. (in press). Análisis bioeconómico de pesquerías críticas. In: Flores, D., P. Sánchez, J.C. Seijo & F. Arreguín (ed.), *Pesquerías Críticas del Golfo de México*. EPOMEX. Serie Científica No. 5.

Seijo, J.C. & O. Defeo. 1994a. Externalidades positivas en pesquerías: la incidencia de interdependencias ecológicas. *Jaina* (México) 5(1): 18.

Seijo, J.C. & O. Defeo. 1994b. Dynamics of resource and fishermen behaviour in coastal invertebrate fisheries. In: Antona, M., J. Catanzano & J. Sutinen (ed.). *Proceedings of the Sixth Conference of the International Institute of Fisheries Economics and Trade*. Paris, Francia. Tomo 1: 209-222.

Seijo, J.C. & D. Fuentes. 1989. The spiny lobster fishery of Punta Allen, Mexico, In: Tietze, U. & P. Merrikin (ed.), *Fisheries Credit Programmes and Revolving Loan Funds: Case Studies*. FAO *Fish. Tech. Pap.* (312): 89-100.

Seijo, J.C., M. Solís & G. Morales. 1987. Simulación bioeconómica de la pesquería de pulpo (*Octopus maya*) de la plataforma continental de Yucatán. In: Ramirez, M. (ed.), *Simposium sobre la Investigación de Biología y Oceanografía Pesqueras en México*, *CICIMAR*, La Paz, B.C.S. México: 125-137.

Seijo, J.C., S. Salas & P. Arceo. 1991a. Marco teórico para el manejo de la pesquería de langosta (*Panulirus argus*) del Golfo de México y Mar Caribe. *Memorias Taller Regional sobre Manejo de la Pesquería de langosta*. ICML/IPN (México): 55-60.

Seijo, J.C., S. Salas, P. Arceo & D. Fuentes. 1991b. Análisis bioeconómico comparativo de la pesquería de langosta *Panulirus argus* de la plataforma continental de Yucatán. *FAO Fish. Rep.* (431): 39-58.

Seijo, J.C., P. Arceo, S. Salas & M. Arce. 1994a. La pesquería de langosta (*Panulirus argus*) de las costas de Yucatán: recursos, usuarios y estrategias de manejo, In: Yañez-Arancibia, A. (ed.), *Recursos Faunísticos del Litoral de la Península de Yucatán*. EPOMEX Serie Científica 2: 33-41.

Seijo, J.C., J.F. Caddy & J. Euán. 1994b. SPATIAL: space-time dynamics in marine fisheries. A software package for sedentary species. *FAO Comp. Inf. Ser. Fish.* (6): 116pp.

Seijo, J.C., O. Defeo & A. de Alava. 1994c. A multiple criterion optimization approach for the management of a multispecies fishery with ecological and technological interdependencies. In: Antona, M., J. Catanzano & J. Sutinen (ed.). *Proceedings of the Sixth Conference of the International Institute of Fisheries Economics and Trade*. Paris, Francia. Tomo 1: 161-167.

Seijo, J.C., O. Novelo & W. Concha. 1996. SIBEC: Simulación bioeconómica de pesquerías. *CINVESTAV-IPN, Unidad Mérida,* Yucatán, México. Laboratorio de Modelación de Pesquerías (software).

Silvert, W. 1982. Top-down modeling in multispecies fisheries. In: Mercer, M.C. (ed.), *Multispecies approaches to fisheries management advice. Can. Spec. Publ. Fish. Aquat. Sci.* 59: 24-47.

Sissenwine, M. 1984a. Why do populations vary?, In: May, R.M. (ed.), *Exploitation of Marine Communities*. Dahlem Konferenzen 1984. Springer-Verlag, Berlin: 59-94.

Sissenwine, M. 1984b. The uncertain environment of fishery scientists and fishery managers. *Mar. Res. Econ.* 1: 1-29.

Sluczanowski, P.R. 1984. A management oriented model of an abalone fishery whose substocks are subject to pulse fishing. *Can. J. Fish. Aquat. Sci.* 41: 1008-1014.

Sluczanowski, P.R. 1986. A disaggregate model for sedentary stocks: the case of South Australian abalone, In: Jamieson, G.S. & N. Bourne (ed.), *North Pacific Workshop on Stock Assessment and Management of Invertebrates*. Can. Spec. Publ. Fish. Aquat. Sci. 92: 393-401.

Smith, A.H. & F.B. Berkes. 1991. Solutions to the "Tragedy of the commons": sea-urchin management in St. Lucia, West Indies. *Environ. Conserv.* 18: 131-136.

Smith, C.L. & R. McKelvey. 1986. Specialist and generalist: roles for coping with variability. *North Am. J. Fish. Manag.* 6: 88-99.

Smith, V.L. 1969. On models of commercial fishing. *J. Polit. Econ.* 77: 181-198.

Sparre, P., E. Ursin & S.C. Venema. 1989. Introduction to tropical fish stock assessment. Part 1 - Manual. *FAO Fish. Tech. Pap.* 306/1: 337 pp.

Squires, D., J. Kirkley & C.A. Tisdell. 1995. Individual transferable quotas as a fisheries management tool. *Rev. Fish. Sci.* 3: 141-169.

Ströbele, W.J. & H. Wacker. 1991. The concept of sustainable yield in multi-species fisheries. *Ecol. Modelling* 53: 61-74.

Sugden, R. & A. Williams. 1978. *The Principles of Practical Cost-Benefit Analysis*. Oxford University Press, Oxford, England.

Sugihara, G., S. Garcia, J.A. Gulland, J.H. Lawton, H. Maske, R.T. Paine, T. Platt, E. Rachor, B.J. Rothschild, E.A. Ursin & B.F.K. Zeitzschel. 1984. Ecosystem dynamics. In: May, R.M. (ed.), *Exploitation of Marine Communities*. Dahlem Konferenzen 1984. Springer-Verlag, Berlin: 131-153.

Sutinen, J.G. & P. Andersen. 1985. The economics of fisheries law enforcement. *Land Econ.* 61: 387-397.

Sutinen, J.G., A. Rieser & J.R. Gauvin. 1990. Measuring and explaining noncompliance in federally managed fisheries. *Ocean Develop. Intern. Law* 21: 335-372.

Verhulst, P.F. 1838. Notice sur la loi que la population suit dans son accroissement. *Corresp. Math. Phys.* 10: 113-121.

Volterra, V. 1926. Fluctuations in the abundance of species, considered mathematically. *Nature* 118: 558-560.

Walters, C.J. 1984. Managing fisheries under biological uncertainty. In: May, R.M. (ed.), *Exploitation of Marine Communities*. Dahlem Konferenzen 1984. Springer-Verlag, Berlín: 263-274.

Walters, C.J. 1986. *Adaptative Management of Renewable Resources*. Macmillian, New York.

Walters, C. 1997. Challenges in adaptive management of riparian and coastal ecosystems. Conservation Ecology [online]1(2):1. Available from the Internet. URL: http://www.consecol.org/vol1/iss2/art1

Walters, C. & A. Parma. 1996. Fixed exploitation rate strategies for coping with effects of climate change. *Can. J. Fish. Aquat. Sci.* 53 : 148-158.

Willmann, W.L. & S.M. Garcia. 1985. A bioeconomic model for the analysis of sequential artisanal and industrial fisheries for tropical shrimp (with a case study of Suriname shrimp fisheries). *FAO Fish. Tech. Pap.* (270): 1-49.

Young, O. 1981. *Natural Resources and the State*. University of Carolina Press, Berkeley, California.

Zar, J.H. 1984. *Biostatistical Analysis*. Prentice-Hall, Englewood Cliffs. New Jersey.

Author Index

Subject Index